THE BATTLE FOR RESILIENCE

UNDERCOVER IN THE ARMY AND ITS REFLECTIONS IN OUR EVERYDAY PSYCHOLOGICAL WELLBEING

The Battle For Resilience: Undercover in the Army and its Reflections in our Everyday Psychological Wellbeing

Spiderwize
Remus House
Coltsfoot Drive
Woodston
Peterborough
PE2 9BF

www.spiderwize.com

A CIP catalogue record for this book is available from the British Library.

ISBN: 978-1-911596-92-9

eBook ISBN: 978-1-911596-93-6

THE BATTLE FOR RESILIENCE

Undercover in the Army and its Reflections in our Everyday Psychological Wellbeing

DR. RUSSELL SHARP

SPIDERWIZE
Peterborough UK
2018

DEDICATIONS

To my wife and daughters for helping me focus and giving so much meaning to my life. I love you.

To my Father, Melvyn Sharp. A true undercover soldier in his final years and in death. Your memory lives on through me and all I do is in your name. You still help me to grow. Thanks Dad. One love.

To family and friends for making me who I am and giving me life.

To Joe and Karen. For the opportunity and support.

To Anthony Squires. Friend and fellow trainee soldier during my time undercover. A good man. Sadly passed away in June 2009 in a car crash leaving loved ones behind. RIP.

www.gonetoosoon.org/memorials/anthony-squires

To all the undercover soldiers – that means you - everyone has their own internal battles hidden from most people.

To all the Linkmen – that means you - everyone makes links with things that are important in their lives.

FOREWORD

We all face a daily battle.

We try our best to negotiate the complex mix of thoughts and feelings we have about ourselves and the world we live in. It is ongoing as we move between the negative and the positive and try to develop ways to meet our psychological needs in a meaningful way that makes us feel good in our naturally chaotic lives.

In short this is a battle for resilience. Resilience can be thought of in different ways. It may be about having many protective factors in place within us and around us so that when adversity or risk comes along it doesn't seem to affect us. It may be about 'bouncing back' to some level of equilibrium when we have faced difficult times. It may also be about personal growth from hidden strengths found, new skills developed or more resources, people, pathways and connections available to support us. Resilience is contextual and depends on the interaction and relationship of an individual and their environment.

Soldiers could be viewed as resilient in many ways, having to be very adaptable in some of the most extreme situations we can face as humans. Physical health is something that is clear to us and we imagine soldiers to be a peak example in this area. Mental health is not as clearly defined, but is as important, if not more for our overall sense of wellbeing in life.

In 2007, I went undercover for six months in the British Infantry to investigate bullying on behalf of the BBC. The 'Undercover Soldier' aired on BBC 1 in 2008. I am currently an Educational Psychologist and this book is the result of many conversations and reflections during the undercover experience and over the following decade after the project. I feel I emerged a different man from the journey and have developed my own resilience. Unique circumstances can lead to unique understandings and through exploring this experience I hope to highlight some key aspects to resilience and how they resonate, link or can be applied to all our lives in everyday situations today. The event has rippled in many ways across the last ten years and I make it relevant to the modern day with recent psychological research and current topics such as social media, body image, gangs, identity, motivation, job satisfaction and fame. The wide eyes of a soldier scanning the horizon after hearing the crack of bullets over their head symbolises as much to me as much as the crack of lead from a pencil of a journalist rapidly noting the overheard words of conspiracy for wrong doing. The fight for survival and the quest for truth are both part of the wider human story.

The book has been split up into chapters surrounding six section battle drills that the Infantry use to co-ordinate pre to post battle. This relates to the story of my pre to post undercover journey with the BBC and the Army. Subheadings show resilience factors that relate to academic research and my real life experiences in the Army.

My old corporal told me when training us in effectively passing messages along a patrol line, 'every man is a linkman'. I was a linkman in Army training, as well as a linkman between two of the largest public sector organisations in the UK (The BBC and the MOD). In a sense we are all 'linkmen' as we find meaning between experiences in our lives and connect to other people. My hope is that you as the reader enjoy the story and related ideas, while making multiple links to your own life.

CONTENTS

INTRODUCTION

CO-INCIDENCE AND OUR RESPONSE

"How on *earth* did you get into that!?"

This is usually the first question everyone asks, whilst wrinkling their brow, when they find out for the first time that I went undercover for six months in the British Army to investigate bullying on behalf of the BBC, resulting in an hour programme on BBC1 and military court cases.

Starting on this road was one of those instances where "the stars either align or they don't" (as the person at the BBC who originally conceived the project said to me after our first meeting back in 2005). Co-incidence and fortune play an invisible, yet crucial part in our psychological well-being. In a chaotic world many factors converge at a particular time and place and without wishing it, you have a new situation to respond to whether you like it or not. We can't control some events that happen to us, but we *can* control how we respond to them.

I was able to put my energies into responding to a chance encounter when it came along. Prima Facie evidence of bullying in the Army had been gathered by the BBC production team from speaking to several people. The Army at that time had a major and acknowledged history around bullying (such as the Deepcut Scandal) although they said they were addressing it. Once legal documents were agreed by BBC lawyers to allow the investigation to proceed, a candidate had to be found who may be able to pull off going undercover in the Army. My name was given to the BBC staff member who was recruiting through a 'friend of a friend'. Some say this is being in the right place at the right time (others joke it was being in the wrong place at the wrong time!). The preliminary 'interview' back in 2005 had been shrouded in mystery, but as I was unemployed after a summer working on a children's camp in America, I thought I would see what it was about. When I was asked questions about going undercover, I sensed it was to do with the Army due to questions about cutting my hair and physical fitness, but I was persuaded I was "a million miles away". I started thinking it might be something to do with drugs or football hooliganism. I went on thinking that for a long time, about a year and a half in-fact as I didn't hear much back following this meeting.

Fast forward to 2007, I had moved on since then and was working as an Inclusion Worker with children, families and schools in Leeds. I got a call to go down to London and meet the producer as they were "now in a position to go ahead with it" (although I didn't know what 'it' was!). At the time, I was in my mid-twenties. I had relatively little job experience and wasn't sure what career would give me the best satisfaction in my life. This is a common feeling for many of us at times and can leave you feeling anxious and vulnerable or it can make you feel ambitious and determined. I was intrigued that this might be my 'opportunity for change' and felt I was fortunate enough to have the skills and resources necessary. Determined to make a good impression I made the effort to go down to London and back in an evening following a normal working day. I had to watch two other documentaries about someone going undercover in the police (Secret Policeman- Mark Daly) and undercover in the BNP (Secret Agent- Jason Gwynne) and write an essay on going undercover in the BBC. I got hounded with more questions about what I might do in certain situations and about me as a person, my history and what I wanted in the future. I didn't quite know what I would be getting involved with, but I was putting my all into getting it because of my frame of mind at the time. A few weeks later I got a call saying they wanted me to come down and they would tell me what it was and see if I was still interested.

When I arrived at the towering London BBC office, I walked up to the reception desk and nervously said who I was there to see. I was escorted to a top floor executive's office with soundproof glass that overlooked the streets of Shepherd's Bush on a typically grey English day. I was left alone for a few minutes and wiped my slightly sweaty palms on the underside of the wooden meeting table I was sitting at. I was thinking, "I'm glad I was wrong with my guess of it being the Army as that would be a lot to put myself though". The Producer I had previously met came into the room and sat down opposite me at the meeting room table. She looked at me and said "I won't beat about the bush, you were right with your guess..." I looked back at her with a slightly surprised, intrigued and whimsical smile and said "oh, which guess...?" She stared back and just said "The Army". I prolonged my surprised, intrigued and whimsical face while in my head one word popped up... "Shit".

She wasn't expecting an answer there and then and I did a lot of walking round and thinking to myself over the next few days after having a lot of the 'ins and outs' of the operation explained to me. There were a lot of 'what if's' and scary ones at that. I beat myself up a bit and spent many a long hour staring at the sky and stars, looking for inspiration by my dad's grave and reflecting on myself and my possible future. Deep down, as soon as I found out what it was, I always knew I was going to say yes.

Well, how could I say no? It felt it was for a good cause if it helped to prevent bullying and improved the lives of young people. It seemed like the most unique life opportunity, was a different challenge and would use skills I felt I had developed. People often make me think back to the moment of saying 'Yes' by asking me questions such as: "Are you glad you did it?", "Would you do it again?", "Was it worth it?", "Are you proud of what you did?". The answers to those questions are filled with semantic, emotional, and perspective ridden complications that make it hard for me to simply answer, as you will find out. Given my views at the time, my character, lessons learned and how it has shaped my frameworks for making sense of the world now, what I can say easily is that: I wouldn't *not* have done it.

Some fortuitous encounters touch only lightly, some leave more lasting effects and some lead people into entirely new life trajectories[1]. As chemist and microbiologist, Louis Pasteur said "Chance favours only the prepared mind". If we have fostered a valued future and have the right optimistic attitude, resources and sense

1 *Bandura, A (1982) The psychology of chance encounters and life paths. American Psychologist, Vol 37(7), 747-755.*

of ourselves as capable, we can maximise the usefulness of chance events to enable our desired life trajectory.

1:

PREPERATION FOR BATTLE

"An invasion of armies can be resisted,
but not an idea whose time has come"

- Victor Hugo, Poet.

OUR IDENTITY AND STORIES

We can all use our 'identity' and the stories we tell about ourselves to go toward meeting some of our basic psychological needs to feel safe and secure and positive about who we are and what we want. Some 'stories' we tell ourselves and others about who we 'are' may be positive or negative and may be intentional or unintentional. The narratives we construct about ourselves in our own head (and in shared conversations with others) have a huge impact on us psychologically. Narrative identity theory says individuals form an identity by integrating their life experiences into an internalised, evolving story of the self, which provides the individual with a sense of unity and purpose in life[2]. This life narrative integrates our reconstructed past, perceived present, and imagined future. The stories can affect how others behave towards us and how we behave towards them. These actions get folded into our sense of self over time and can help confirm or deny certain narratives about our identity. For our sense of resilience, it's important we can reflect on the stories about ourselves and have some opportunities to have an impact on how they are authored.

I couldn't think about setting foot into a recruitment office until I had a double identity to protect my 'real self' from being discovered when I was in the Army. The start of creating my double identity or new 'life story' was to tell friends and work mates that I wanted to join the Army. I'd never previously mentioned or talked about this with anyone or had any real urge to join the Army when I was younger. Telling friends was two-fold:

---

2 *McAdams, D (2001). The psychology of life stories. Review of General Psychology 5 (2): 100–122. doi:10.1037/1089-2680.5.2.100.*

1) It meant they knew where I was going so if the Army checked or spoke to any of them it would all join up and seem 'real'.

2) If I could convince my closest friends I wanted to join the Army, I knew I could convince the Army.

This was the first emotionally challenging situation during the project. As you can imagine, having never talked about the Army and being on a career path to an Educational Psychologist, I got a variety of reactions from friends! People's mouths and eyes did different things. There were those who would nod along and smile even though I could tell they were thinking I had gone crazy. There were those who were genuinely supportive and backed me if it was what I wanted. There were the ones who slapped me round the face and wondered why I was 'throwing away' my education and potential career. I was thankful for the ones who were supportive (genuinely or not) as it made it so much easier at the time. I was even more grateful for the ones who gave me all the hassle about what I was doing as even though they made it difficult at the time, they were looking out for my interest when they didn't have the full picture.

My favourite reactions from my friends when I told them I was joining the Army included:

*"You're having my F**king eyes out?!"*

"You're going to get shot to shit"

"Is it because you're fed up of working with women all the time?!"

Despite the varied reactions I always kept in my mind that one day I would (hopefully) be able to tell them what I was really doing, which helped.

I really wanted to tell some of my best friends the whole thing - many times. The time I came closest was Christmas 2007 after I had a few drinks and one of my best friends started talking about the BBC. I literally opened my mouth to say 'well guess what...', but we were interrupted by another drunken friend shouting loudly, full of Christmas cheer. The moment passed and I thought it best not to tell them, even though I wanted to and I trusted them. It's one of those things where you tell your one best friend innocently and swear them to secrecy; they say they won't tell, but have to tell their other best friend and swear them to secrecy; who then tells their best friend; who knows so-and-so; who is friends with what's-his-face; who just happens to have an uncle who turns out to be working in the Army where I am. Close family had another story, and for a year and a half I had to keep various groups separate as I didn't want inconsistencies to appear in stories about where I was and what I was doing. This was a drain on the memory having to remember who I had said what to.

My 'story' got much easier as I went along telling people and I realised how powerful '*making your memories real*' can be in creating an 'identity' (much like an actor). I had no memories of wanting to join the army as I had never thought about it, so I had to create some. I took any small aspect that was true to me (such as enjoying physical activity) and emphasised it in my mind as a reason I wanted to join the Army. I pictured myself as a child surrounded by Army paraphernalia, toy tanks, paper fighter planes and plastic guns. I imagined playing with them all while putting mud on my face as if it was my dream to join the Army. I convinced myself I wanted to join and I had always wanted to join. If I convinced myself, then no-one could catch me out from anything I said. Memories are recollections of sounds, sights, smells and other sensations or feelings of particular moments in the past. That moment is no longer the physical present whether it was at one time 'real' or not. Memories of physical actions and experiences and fabrication of these events are both experienced at the level of the brain. They can both be recalled when asked about it. So having previously contemplated experiences in fine detail, I had made some 'real' memories which would hopefully be automatically conveyed through me without me having to feel nervous and create a history for myself on the spot.

Although I was doing the above to be purposefully deceitful, we can manage other's impressions of us and our impressions of ourselves to our advantage through positive stories (and actions), kindness and noticing of strengths. Having opportunity to give voice to your own preferred identity and feel you have at least some impact on shaping it in a positive way in a social world is essential for our own esteem and psychological wellbeing. This very book is perhaps in part something I was driven to write to extend and re-voice my own identity around a complex event with many of the rich details not being in the public narrative around it.

INCREASING TRANSFERABLE KNOWLEDGE AND SKILLS

Soldiers stock up on ammunition before battle. We can build up our own brain's 'ammunition' by continuing to learn throughout our life. There are always new skills and knowledge bases that can be useful in many walks of life and transferable to different contexts. We can shy away from new training or learning new information as we can feel it's too hard to learn new things or it's not relevant to us. This is one psychological barrier to overcome in order to help us be more resilient. It's helpful to have more knowledge and skills than our particular current occupational label suggests we need. You never know what you may need to adapt to a situation as a human making your way in a changeable world.

With my story down and my new 'willingness' to go and join the Infantry, it was time to start learning all about investigative journalism and TV production. The BBC enlisted me in a lot of in-house training to get me up to speed. A lot of the courses I did had a double reason for doing them. For instance I was on a risk management course- not for just for risk managing TV production, but for risk managing myself while I was in the Army. I had practical law sessions, first aid sessions, safe handling sessions, multiple journalism courses and investigative research input.

One part of BBC training that I found incredibly useful (and a whole heap of fun) was 'Hostile Environments training' used for journalist who go to dangerous places and report on things like war. At the time this was the closest experience I had to being in a military type environment without actually being in one. This was a very intensive training course and you learn all sorts; including how to run from handgun fire, how to probe the ground for mines, how to do extreme first aid with blown off limbs and chest wounds, how to manage confrontational border crossings and even how to attempt to survive kidnap and interrogation. They loved to surprise you with pyrotechnics and make the training simulations as real as possible. It culminates in a final day tour into an actual military training facility and a whole day of role play set up using real life soldiers as terrorists, enemies and associates. In many ways the surprises, anticipation of them and mock kidnapping we faced here were psychologically scarier than most things that happened in Army training. Although with several middle class journalists doing the course it was no-where near as physically demanding as the real Army!

I was fortunate enough to have an Investigative Journalism Masterclass with Nick Davis - British investigative journalist, writer and documentary maker who was responsible for uncovering the News of the World phone hacking affair. I learned various things in this class that help me in my current job as an Educational Psychologist and generally in life. One key lesson that stuck with me and really helped me when I was undercover was what to do with that feeling we all have when something just doesn't quite add up. You may be in a conversation and someone says something that feels like it contradicts something else, or may behave in a certain way that you don't expect. It's a feeling sort of like the moment in the film 'The Matrix' when Neo sees a black cat do the same thing twice. It's also like when you are reading and turn over two pages at once without realising. Your brain feels like it's missed a step and it goes 'huh'. Nick's main point was that these feelings are important to be listened to and followed up on, rather than be dismissed or ignored. Nick Davis uses these moments to go deeper than the overt, obvious news story and investigate the more interesting one that is being concealed behind it all.

Our brains are very clever at making patterns in the world[3]. When our sub-conscious can't fluidly link together pieces of information we have, we pause and try to understand why something feels amiss. What happens normally then, is that we just shrug and carry on with what we were doing assuming there must be something wrong with us, what happened was unimportant or we have missed some piece of information in the past that doesn't matter. We rarely stop to realise we feel this way because there is something missing from the picture -or more to the point- there might be a piece of the pattern that is hidden from us for various reasons. We have all been in a situation where someone has acted strangely and we've wondered why, only to later find out they didn't want us to know about something that was on the verge of being discovered. We can use this understanding of our brains as 'pattern makers' to our advantage to help us be more aware of complex situations. I used it in the Army to get a sense of what shouldn't be happening or was being covered up. I use it as an Educational Psychologist to understand the underlying history behind the relationships and behaviours between school staff, young people and families. I use it as a human to be kind and sensitive to people I interact with when I get

---

3 *For interesting thoughts on 'thin slicing' and the psychology behind our pattern making read 'Blink'- Malcom Gladwell*

a sense that there are other things going on in their life that might be making them behave unusually or not be feeling as good as they could. This extra level of awareness and understanding in our interactions with others helps strengthen our relationships, which in turn strengthens our resilience.

LEARNING FROM OUR MISTAKES

Practice is essential for developing our confidence and skill in any particular area. No-one who is top of their field in any discipline ever made it there by talent or innate ability alone. They practiced hard over and over again. We may feel we are not particularly good at something if it's the first time we have done it and may therefore stop, trying to avoid feeling negative. Overcoming this is a key factor to being resilient. Learning through mistakes is part of a 'growth mind-set'. This way of thinking can help us thrive on challenge and see 'failure' not as evidence of unintelligence or inability, but as a heartening springboard for developing and stretching our existing abilities[4].

My first ever go with a secret camera is shown in the BBC programme. It's just me trying to film myself in-front of a mirror while holding what looked like some sort of file-o-fax or CD folder. It was trickier than you think at first and I am a sucker for perfection (as was the production team), so I had to practice until I was spot on. When practicing with secret cameras I was able to identify and apply some existing transferable skills and knowledge I had. I had many years of doing magic tricks as a hobby and briefly as an amateur job. This meant I was used to

4 *Dweck, C. S. (2006). Mindset: The new psychology of success. New York: Random House. Chicago*

holding things in a relaxed manner while being aware of which angle they were facing, what someone would see if they looked at it, how to misdirect attention if necessary, sleight of hand and building rapport[5]. This gave me some confidence in handling the cameras beyond the training I received. On top of handling and using the cameras, I had to be able to combine my journalism training of asking the right questions to reveal key information as well as accurately filming people's faces and reactions, while maintaining my cover story and holding a 'normal' conversation. Not an easy task by any means. To continue to practice this, the production team set up a series of tasks that combined these skills to get me ready for the real thing. As uncomfortable (and sometimes amusing) as they were at the time, they were valuable for my learning and through the mistakes and fumbles, I developed this skill.

I practiced role playing real life situations with the production team and at the start asked lots of odd questions and fumbled around with the bag I was holding (that was a camera), putting it in some places you probably wouldn't naturally put a bag. I got tangled in lots of information I created on the spot about myself when asked questions about who I was. I bumbled my way through the first practice scenario with a flustered and confused story about myself. Further to that, I wasn't

---

5 *For good reference books on card handling and/or misdirection and/or useful magic theory, some books that have influenced me are: Hugard & Braue- Expert card technique, Luke Jermay-3510, Corinda- Thirteen steps to Mentalism, Derren Brown- Devils picture book series and most of his work. Most work by Andy Nyman and David Berglas are also essential for background knowledge and theory of perception, presentation and practice of psychological magic.*

getting good camera shots or audio of what was being said as I had put the camera near a speaker with loud music. Epic Fail!

My next few attempts varied in their situations and I felt my own confidence increase the more I did. I practiced using shirt cameras and bag cameras in different places to help my training. I also practiced filming sequences and getting general shots of the environment I was in that would cut together to make a coherent story for a television viewer to understand.

Beyond practicing with the camera, I even did a few tasks just to increase my ice breaking and confidence with small talk. I pretended I was a professional basketball player, a business manager, a zoo keeper who looked after apes at London zoo and even a trainee astronaut. Despite its playful veneer and the dubiousness of developing my ability to deceive, this training was deadly serious as consequences of me getting it wrong in the Army were potentially disastrous.

My final few training sessions used the actual secret cameras I would use in the Army. I conditioned myself into rituals of how to use them while looking normal and continuing my relationship building. I was even secretly filmed myself while practicing with the production team. The experience really helped me with understanding feelings of what it's like to be secretly filmed and what one goes through when they find out.

This skill development in a short space of time shows the importance of 'failure' and acceptance of this as a key part of learning. If you feel you can't do something, reframe it as you can't do it *yet*. As humans, we can learn and we don't have a fixed skill-set. We are resilient because we can change and develop.

SPENDING SOME TIME WITH YOURSELF

We are social creatures by nature and it's good to have support networks, but in terms of building ourselves as resilient people, it can be positive to spend a short amount of time living independently to develop the skills you need to live this way if forced into it at some point in life due to unforeseen events or loss. It's also important to have time to reflect on you and your life and discover new things about yourself. Living alone can give you time to try new hobbies and develop creative ideas that may otherwise not get chance to grow. It can also be scary and lonely, but if we avoid it for these reasons we may lose some opportunity for important personal growth.

I had a whole life in London that no one knew about apart from the production team and I spent a lot of time disconnected from my usual life. When it came to background checks to get into the Army we couldn't have anything linking the name Russell Sharp to the BBC. So for all this initial BBC training, I was given (for no special reasons) the name of David James. Dave for short! I rehearsed saying I was Dave so many times until it became natural in any BBC environment, but still had to watch my tongue at times. The team I was working closely with at the BBC even called me Dave to be on the safe side. In this environment it was used so much that when we could finally use my real name again it actually sounded wrong in this context, even to me. My name Dave became so engrained that it started to cross over to my real personal life. I remember being sat at a friend's house party and there being a person there who was actually called Dave. Anytime someone said his name my head would automatically turn to look who wanted me, before quickly turning back as I realised- I'm *not* Dave!

By this time in my pre-undercover training, I was living in London during the week and coming back to Leeds at the weekends to see friends and make it look like I was still around and everything was normal. The BBC had a nice apartment they kindly rented for me in Ealing, West London. I had lived away from home before at university, but never totally alone or as far away from family.

When I wasn't practicing filming, or living independently, I was working on fitness at a gym and in various parks. Walpole Park in Ealing was a place I regularly ran round. I had the good fortune to be there in the summer so I could make the most of circling the park four or five times in the sunny warm evenings. There was also a jazz and comedy festival on for a couple of weeks that was just the thing to help me relax and briefly take my mind off what was ahead. I enjoyed the time to reflect in this park about what I was doing, why and what I wanted to do in the future. The additional fitness work I did in a nearby gym was mainly to strengthen my joints so I reduced risk of injury in training. Injury could have spelt trouble for the investigation. My personal trainer at the Gym even called me Dave too! I often wonder if these people who met 'Dave' ever saw the programme and realised what I was really doing when I met them.

My 'camouflage' down in London went to extreme lengths. I left no electronic footprint down there, just in-case the Army suspected anything and looked into my background. If they did, they would only have seen my open history and no links to the BBC- or even hardly to London. I didn't use my debit card in London and I didn't use my mobile phone in and around any BBC office and had several unregistered mobile phones for talking to different sets of people (as either Russell or Dave!). I think at one point I had five mobile phones I carried around and I needed to remember who 'I' was on each of them. We were ultra-cautious and even if anyone had hacked 'Russell Sharp's' phone, they would only have heard me talking about normal things. I didn't use my personal e-mail in any BBC offices and I kept myself to myself as much as possible. I even had to use the back entrance of the BBC office I was working in, just so the security guard didn't get used to seeing my face every day in case he had any military connections. This may all seem a bit extreme, but this was the dedication of the production team to the cause. It had to be perfect or not at all. I was happy that every attempt to reduce any chance of a leak of information could save my bacon. I looked at it as constructive paranoia. This constructive paranoia and caution did come at a slight cost though. It started to invade my dreams. I had one dream that when I made it into the Army, I was taken aside on the first day. A big Platoon Commander said "Sharp- into this office". As I walked in and sat down in a cold hard steel chair, the platoon commander said nonchalantly; "we know you work for the BBC". In the dream I was scared, but I maintained a face of blissful ignorance and looked back at them as if to say 'what on earth are you talking about'.

The Platoon Commander then leaned towards me, stared at me and put a covert surveillance picture of me walking into a BBC building on the table and repeated in a sterner, all-knowing voice: "We know you work for the BBC".

You could regard all this covert and secret camera stuff as quite 'cool', but many times the reality is a bit of a lonely, cold, calculated and distant existence. For a short amount of time though, having time to focus on you is a beneficial exercise. I had written off four months before the Army (and a lot of my time in the Army), knowing that I would be relatively isolated. In today's constantly connected world, finding solitude for short spells can bring psychological benefits including being free from distractions to concentrate on your own thoughts and focus on practising what you want to develop.

HAVING THE RIGHT TOOLS

Humans have always developed tools to overcome our physical limitations and help us find more efficient ways to live. Whether it's the stone tools of cavemen or the space shuttle of NASA, we stand out in our ability from other species to develop the tools to help us do what we need to flourish. We certainly benefit more than ever from increased technology and gadgets that help us with almost every task imaginable. There are some cases where having too many tools can prevent us from learning valuable independent skills, but picking the *right* tools for us can go to extending our resilience.

There was no way conventional secret cameras would have worked in the Army. Shirt cameras were a no go due to very close inspections by military staff, constant changing of clothes at a moment's notice and of course the problem of crawling through mud and rivers in what you are wearing! It would have been a criminal offence to try and destroy military property and put a camera in something like a bag, so we couldn't do that. We had to build secret cameras out of everyday objects that I could take in, would look normal and could be briefly handled without being obvious that it was different. I also had little nooks and crannies in various essential items where I could hide memory cards safely once I had recorded something important. They were all made so that even if you picked them up and looked at them closely, you wouldn't really notice anything. You may have spotted a hole in a strange place or a lump that shouldn't be there, but unless you suspected the object to be something other than what it looked like, you wouldn't be able to tell. I took comfort in this and it meant I could leave these things in plain view and not worry. I didn't leave them lying around too much though when I wasn't there just in case!

The only other two pieces of equipment that were essential to me (and probably got the most use of any items) were my phone and my diary. They were far from just a phone and a diary though. These would become my weapons, my ritualistic tokens, my evidence, my friends and even an extension of me. The guys who had made my other secret cameras found a way to cut the circuitry in the phone so that no red light showed when the phone was recording a video. The phone was only ever intended to be a backup to the actual secret cameras should they fail. We shall see later, due to circumstance and the environment I was in, the phone became my main weapon of choice and the simple cutting of the circuitry was one of the most important factors in the investigation working.

It always helps to have the right tools for the job. As humans, we can craft and try different tools to make our life easier and achieve things we wouldn't ordinarily be able to do. We continue our resilience as a species by creating ways to adapt our environment to us and overcome any physical limitations we have.

COMMUNICATION

Communication is an innate need of ours as a social species and we have developed many ways to do so, helping us thrive and extend our thinking and understanding about ourselves and the world. A lack of communication pathways and ability can mean we become stuck in our internal battles and end up feeling anxious, trapped and isolated. It's essential for our mental health to be able to communicate safely about our thoughts and feelings to move forward in a positive way. We also need to have the tools to communicate, whether this be through spoken language, non-verbal gesture and behaviour, signs, use of technology or otherwise. The greater the ability we have to articulate well what we want to communicate and the better others are at trying to be receptive to this, the more resilient we are as people.

I was going into a solitary, secure environment. I would have to stay in that environment for long periods of time and I wasn't sure how I would be able to communicate with the production team and let them know what's going on or if I was ok. I hoped I would be allowed to use my phone inside to make calls or send text or media messages, but I had no way to tell what reception would be like or how often I would be able to use my phone, if I was even allowed to have one.

With the lack of ability to check back with BBC colleagues, I had to memorise many previous Army allegations, evidence and investigations that linked to bullying. This meant if I heard any key names while I was there I could hopefully put two and two together and not miss something. I spent days going through all the prima facie evidence the BBC had collected and being tested on it. I created my own mantras about getting facts and corroboration of events and how to handle my journalistic enquiries that evolved from all my training courses and speaking to successful journalists. I memorised key mobile numbers of the production team and a lawyer's personal mobile in case I needed them. We didn't want them on my phone while I was there in case I got caught or it got taken. I even came up with complex codes for text messages or e-mails if we thought what I sent out was being surveyed. I drew on my old magic hobby again for this one and found a list of codes that 'psychics' use when divining information from an audience with the help of an assistant.

There was a lot of planning for the worst case scenario. It was scary to contemplate everything that might happen to me from broken bones, to being found out, to being put in military prison, to beatings, hiding in fields, or legging it over fences to a predetermined rendezvous point until I can be picked up by a team member. One small accident on a live firing range could also have resulted in my death. These scenarios weren't nice to contemplate, but I'm glad we had plans for most serious eventualities, just in case. They say the boy scouts are always prepared, but they didn't have anything on us! It was also a comfort that I had a BBC legal team behind me willing to do everything they could. I had to put a lot of trust in them. They told me what I could and couldn't do to comply with legal and ethical guidelines in the investigation and what they could legally protect me from. With everyone I worked with throughout, I did feel they all put my safety as an ultimate priority over their own business or personal objectives. In the event of a lot of the worst case scenarios happening, the production team took it in weekly shifts to stay in a town fairly near to where I was, just so someone was closer than London at all times. It was some comfort to know I had allies not a million miles away.

It felt better to be overprepared than underprepared. The communication options I had helped me feel more secure, not worry and get on with my job. The more communication pathways we have in life, the more we can problem solve, talk through our thoughts, connect to others and understand about the world.

POSITIVE RELATIONSHIPS AND LOVE

You can't do everything yourself. The greater your networks of support, the easier life is and the more resilient we can be. Positive relationships are perhaps the single most important factor in our overall psychological well-being[6]. They provide us with emotional support and containment, meet our communication and social interaction needs and they help us develop secure attachments that in turn allow us to explore and learn about the world. They also provide us access to a range of skills, knowledge and abilities we can draw on by extension.

---

6 *Luthar, S. S. (2006). Resilience in development: A synthesis of research across five decades. In D. Cicchetti & D. J. Cohen (Eds.), Developmental psychopathology (Risk, disorder, and adaptation 2nd ed., Vol. 3, pp. 739 795). Hoboken, NJ: Wiley.*

I would never have been able to do what I did had I not had the support of a dedicated and hard-working team. I did need one 'specialist' tool to be able to tie my cover story, communication with the BBC and recording of information all together. What I needed...was a girlfriend!

Having a girlfriend would be my excuse for using my phone a lot, someone visiting to film me and all sorts of other communication and strategic tactics. The colleague who agreed to the role wasn't called Susan, but the production team decided this would be my girlfriend's name.

So the beautiful and romantic story of Russell and Susan began. They met in O'Neill's bar in London, just near Oxford Street Tube (where we had actually gone to meet as work colleagues). They were introduced through friends and just hit it off straight away. Russell wrote a lot about his feelings for Susan in his diary that went into the Army. Russell even e-mailed Susan a lot before the Army and they had conversations about all sorts of wonderful things in life as well as a bit of an argument because Susan didn't really want Russell to join the Army. She loved him and didn't want anything to happen to him. Russell loved Susan as well, but joining the Army had been his life-long dream and he hoped Susan would understand. She did. Russell even memorised Susan's address so he could send her letters from within the Army if he wanted to.

A sickly cute and twisted love story! Susan was a bit of a peculiar being at times. She sometimes took the physical form of the female BBC colleague who people in the Army saw. She often sounded rather like a set of BBC male colleagues on the other end of e-mail or phone texts trying their best to respond in a way they thought a female may respond to information or conversation. Susan was also members of the production team on the end of phone calls when I was in the Army who I could tell about my day's events, how I was and things I had seen. Susan was a mix of my real memories of previous relationships, girls I had got close to and moments we had shared. Susan helped me get into the Army and ended up being my main way out of the Army. She made me lie sometimes and made people feel things for me, such as sympathy, which I wished they didn't. Susan gave me hope when I despaired at being in the Army for so long. Susan got me though the investigation in so many ways I don't think I even know them all. Susan was a beautiful gestalt entity who consisted of a concoction of real, contextual, false and fabricated memories, meanings and modes. I may well refer to 'Susan' in the rest of this book. When I do, you may have to work out what part of the concept of 'Susan' I am using and for which purpose. We shared a love on many levels.

Love can be confusing for the human mind and you can often not know what is real and what may be a construct. We have all had internal battles in our real life relationships and have considered what 'love' may be for us. Love can be the most powerful factor in giving us hope and a reason to live. We can think we are in 'love' with someone when we are in a vulnerable place ourselves, but that this may just be an attachment we have made that meets some of our underlying psychological needs. We can often be too easily distracting into searching for 'love' with what society tells us it should be. To have a long lasting resilient and loving relationship with an individual, it's important to develop that feeling over time when you are in a positive frame of mind and crucially can feel like you are yourself around them. Loving ourselves can help us love others in a more complete way.

BEING TRUE TO YOURSELF

'Being yourself' is not only a key factor in a successful undercover operatives mission, but something that is key for our wellbeing in everyday life. If we have to alter our behaviour to meet other people's expectations of us, we will continue to not feel connected to others and ourselves. It can take guts to 'be yourself' around others if you feel social pressures or don't feel safe, but often the results of not being true to how we think and feel can cause us to develop a web of lies that only further constrains us and makes us feel low. People warm to others who are comfortable with themselves. We can find common interests with anyone as we are all human at the end of the day, so there is no need to pretend to be something you are not to relate to others.

Despite the obvious irony of me not being who I said I was, within the implicit deceit of being undercover, I learned the importance of still being true to yourself. In reality all the above BBC training was happening at the same time as the Army recruitment process. Recruitment takes a long time - three to four months. I split the story up for clarity. My overall orders were simple:

- Get into the Army.
- If you see or hear of anything that breaks the Army's own guidelines on bullying then report it and try and record it (Safely).
- Get out of the Army (Safely).

These were my original orders and the ones I stuck to. As the saying goes, 'easier said than done'!

The moment I walked into the Army recruitment office in Leeds, I set the ball rolling. The first visit wasn't so bad and I was in and out in five minutes after expressing my interest to join the Infantry and do basic training at Catterick. The reason I had to go here is because this was the place where most accusations, stories and evidence of bullying appeared in the prima facie evidence collected by the BBC.

Every time I walked out the recruitment office or the Army barracks, I felt like the character Keyser Söze played by Kevin Spacey in the film the Usual Suspects. You know the part at the end where he walks out of the police building with a pronounced limp and slowly corrects his walk, his eyes narrow and he lights a cigarette appearing calm and collected in the knowledge that only he knows what's really happening. That felt like me going from army crazed raw recruit to trained undercover reporter as I went in and out of the recruitment office.

The first test of my identity came without me expecting it. The corporal dealing with me at the recruitment office had been very friendly up until this point. Without warning, he sat down, leaned forward quickly, folded his arms, glared at me and said in a stern voice: "So, why don't you want to be an officer". It was like time passed in slow motion and I split myself into two parts. One part was recollecting the memories I had created and made to feel real and one part was analysing the non-verbal body signals I was sending out (tense twitches, face reddening, throat gulps, too much or too little eye contact etc.). I called it a 'dual reality' technique. I became very adept at this skill during my whole experience and was able to be aware of how I was coming across to other people as well as interacting with or recollecting my fabricated memories in a way that felt as if they were my actual history. It was like the front of my body was a shield for them to see everything was 'fine', while the back of my body was firing with thoughts, but hiding it all from view. When he asked me, I had convinced myself so much that I wanted to join the Army that I almost genuinely felt confused as to why he may ask. This same subtle inquiry into who I was occurred quite a few more times along my journey and I tried to use the same 'dual reality' technique in response.

So, following a significant amount of brain activity in less than a second, I gave the reason for not wanting to be an officer. I said although I had always wanted to be in the Army, I wanted to go from ground level up to understand the Army fully. I also said I didn't want my university degree to make me just 'waltz' in above people and I also wasn't very confident or comfortable with ordering people about. He heard my responses and didn't say much else. He invited me back for the next stage. I shook the hand of the Corporal when I left the office to appear confident, although I saw out of the corner of my eye he wiped his hand on his trousers after. I guess I couldn't control the sweat from my palms in that tense situation. I made a mental note not to do that again!

The next visit involved a cognitive test. The score on this depended on what career option within the Army you had access to and what training bases you may therefore be sent to. As the production team needed me to go to the Infantry in Catterick, where most of the evidence was, we decided I should try and do less well than I potentially could on any tests of ability. We didn't want officer training in Sandhurst to be an option. So, I sat down at the touch screen test thinking this was probably the only time when the less I try and the worse I do, the better the result! Or so I thought! It was a timed test, but I took my time answering being under no pressure to do well. I aimed to try and get about 50% right and then just make small mistakes on other items. When the results came back I had done very poorly. Much worse than I meant to do! I had underestimated the weighting of the score on the speed with which you answer. The corporal who gave me the results said he couldn't understand it as I had scored the same as the previous candidate who had left school with a few GCSEs and I was sat there with my psychology degree performing at the same level. Doh! So much for not drawing attention to myself! I quickly came up with a story (which was partially true) that I didn't realise it was a timed test so I was taking my time in answering and perhaps some questions must have recorded zero as I took too long. I felt like this sort of made sense when I said it. He still wanted me to retest in a month so I had more career options open to me. Fortunately, joining the infantry was still a choice with my current results. I said I wanted to do this anyway and not bother with a re-test and he reluctantly said ok. I had just about got away with it. I made a note to myself to never try and cheat tests or cheat who I really was. I did have a degree and I wasn't hiding that. I thought I am who I am, so I will make myself fit in and not change who I am. You are more likely to be found out or look strange if it's something you don't naturally do. For example, if you don't smoke normally- don't smoke to fit in. If you need to talk to the people who smoke, make them buy into you for who you really are. A good example of this is when I didn't have to join in racist discussions for people to accept me in a conversation that was full of racially derogatory comments. Following one particularly racist conversation, I was prompted by a fellow recruit to say 'Paki'. "Go on Sharp, say it" a recruit said (referring to the 'P' word). "It", I replied. A classic childhood gag had helped me out in this instance and I didn't have to change how I wanted to act for them to continue to utter all sorts of comments in-front of me.

It can be a difficult moment when a group you are part of are openly forcing you to join in with them and what they are asking conflicts with your moral or ethical values. Some may drop these values in favour of fitting in, but there is no need if you are true to yourself. You can find common interests and connections with anyone, even if at first there appears to be significant differences. At the end of the day we are all human.

I had one last interview in Leeds with a high ranking officer. He said I had the 'golden ticket' with a degree and tried very hard to persuade me again to be an officer. He also said if I really wanted to be a combat infantryman then he would be fine with that. Against the advice of the production team to be dead set in my thinking, in the moment I felt it best to look indecisive and go away from that meeting to have 'thinking time' about what I should do, just to show I was listening to them and I was taking them seriously. Of course, after my 'thinking time' there was only one choice: a soldier in the infantry please!

I made it to Army selection.

2:

REACTION TO EFFECTIVE ENEMY FIRE

"If you know the enemy and know yourself, you need not fear the result of a hundred battles. If you know yourself but not the enemy, for every victory gained you will also suffer a defeat. If you know neither the enemy nor yourself, you will succumb in every battle."

– *Sun Tzu, Chinese military strategist and philosopher.*

SELF-REGULATION

It's easy to lose our self-discipline and let strong emotions rule our behaviour. It's important to be in touch with how we are feeling, but we also need some strategies to regulate these emotions in order to help us manage daily events and remain in control. Managing these feelings can allow us to remain safe, carefully consider options and choose our actions carefully based on value and reason rather than acting impulsively, which can lead to events we regret.

The autonomic nervous system works to keep order below the level of our awareness. It regulates and balances many automatic functions of our bodies, including emotions. One of the most important functions it regulates is our automatic, instinctive response to perceived threats in the environment. Our threat response system determines whether we are angry and want to fight, or scared and want to flee, or hunker down until the threat passes (freeze). This is known as the fight, flight, or freeze response. There are times when we want our fight or flight response to be in control and a solider in battle is a perfect example of this. It is a normal response to feeling unsafe. There are times when these responses are out of balance and proportion with our environment, we are not self-regulating well and we experience symptoms such as anxiety. Awareness and understanding of these emotions are important to be present in the moment and make these natural responses work positively for you.

Army Selection took place in Edinburgh. I was anxious through this time as everything was new and unpredictable in an unfamiliar context. Two days of physical tests, medicals, introductory military lessons and team activities where corporals were watching to see how you performed.

The investigation had started so no matter how I was feeling, I had to overcome this by throwing myself whole heartedly into the tasks we were given. We were quickly transformed from a "bunch of layabouts" in our tracksuits, to a set of young men who stood up straight. There were fitness tests to pass with a set limit of push-ups, chin ups and sit ups as well as being able to run a mile and a half in under 10:30. I got the second best time in the mile and a half run that day, which I was slightly disappointed about due to my competitive streak, but just gave me more motivation to beat the winner next time. We took part in team building activities and some lessons about grenades. During this time I kept the role of the 'grey man'- i.e. I didn't fall behind or stand out too much, wasn't the centre of attention but got involved with games and chat, asked some questions to look interested but not too many to be a pain. I generally just kept my head down and got on with what I was supposed to be doing. I also had to have a full medical, which was good for my own peace of mind that I was working ok!

It was a pressure situation and many didn't make it either on physical grounds, or attitude grounds as they 'acted up' or 'mouthed off' showing their lack of strategies to control themselves when feeling uneasy. It was evident which candidates had an element of self-discipline at the first overnight stay, when there was a split between those preparing for the next day and trying to get some sleep and those who spent the night caught in a game of 'one up man ship' to see who could do the loudest prank or stupidest dare. Unsurprisingly, the main culprits for the night disturbance were the ones who didn't make it through to the Army. These young men may have been anxious in their own way in a large male group away from their comfort zone, but without a developed level of emotional resilience, they were not able to make these emotions work effectively for them in this context.

I had a final interview at the end of selection to determine whether I had passed or not. The investigation could have been over before it had really begun at this point. I had a long nervous wait in a cold blue waiting room. A corporal was keeping an eye on everyone and occasionally chirped up with insulting comments about us, knowing we had to politely accept whatever he said. I just kept going through my story and kept focussed on going in and making the right impression.

It paid off. The interviewing officer asked me simple questions and didn't go into any real depth about my history or why I wanted to be there. He did mention my degree and I had to tell him why I didn't want to be an officer (yet). Helpfully for me he said that reports from the team activities showed that I hadn't taken charge of enough situations to show officer potential yet. This was music to my ears and meant my deliberate actions to hang back in team activities had worked. It also meant if I got questioned in the future about why I didn't want to be an officer, I had good reasoning to demonstrate why it wasn't right for me. He shook my hand and gave me a certificate. I was accepted.

Until this point, I honestly hadn't felt overly worried about anything as this is what I had been preparing for. Perhaps I had just been so busy it hadn't really hit home what I was about to do. Passing the attestation point where

I was legally signed up to the Army and couldn't easily walk away was a point where I needed to greatly draw on my own abilities to regulate my emotions. The week before I went in was the most tense for me. I made the mistake of watching the film 'Full Metal Jacket'. This left me with a lot of scary thoughts about what may happen to me or what I may have to face or deal with. If you happen to be about to join the Army, don't watch this film! Although I can say, from my experience, life in general in the British Infantry training programme is not very similar.

Three days to go and I was getting very anxious. I kept having grand notions of my life changing forever that we all tend to have before significant events, not realising that although things around you may be different, core elements of yourself and your life don't change. I sat on the grass for a long time in these evenings in Walpole Park in Ealing where I had done so much of my physical and mental training. The park had become a sort of reflective and spiritual base for the whole adventure I would embark on. I watched the birds flying and people playing. I looked at autumn colours on the trees and parkland while listening to certain songs I found moving on my I-pod. I noticed myself breathing fresh air and was happy just staring at the world go by. I made an effort to be present in the moment and enjoy it. This was a good calming strategy to help me regulate my feelings and I make the effort to apply this in every day contexts. I was keen to enjoy normality and freedom before it was metaphorically snatched away from me for a while.

The second to last day doing last minute checks with the production team was hectic. We had done all we could have done, but kept going over everything, just in case. At an office in London we spent until midnight packing my bag perfectly with all I may need and putting the secret cameras in places they may not look, but didn't matter if they did. It was time for control of the operation to be predominantly in my hands. There were hugs, best luck wishes and a few watery eyes from the production team. They had put a lot of their lives into this before I got on board, in some cases years, so this was a big moment for them. We were all emotionally involved.

I spent my last night at home with family. I slept better than I thought I would. The sun rose on the morning of the 21st of October 2007 and it was time. It was extremely difficult saying goodbye to my family on that morning. I didn't really speak after a hug. It felt like I had a knife in my throat. The drive to the station went too quickly and I kept wishing for time to stop. Time in general felt it was going fast because my senses were heightened, but it felt like whatever I looked at was moving slowly. A green and grey blur kept going past the window while I was aware of the noise of the radio and the interior of the car I was sat in.

On the train to Darlington to be picked up by the Army, I felt sick and at a peak of nervousness. I can't remember what I was thinking, which probably says something for my state of mind at the time! This was only lessened by having to record a piece to camera in the toilets about how I felt. A member of my production crew was on the same train and came up with a clever ploy to leave a covert camera in there for me. I saw the rest of my production crew on this day, although I couldn't speak to them as they were disguised as members of the public to secretly film me setting off on the coach to the Army Barracks.

We finally came across the big iron gates. Armed military personal guarding the gate stopped us and stared at us for a moment. The gates opened and the way into camp was clear.

I had arrived in the Army.

I paused, staring out the coach window at the welcome sign and made deliberate movements to make sure my bag was zipped up. I bent down and firmly grabbed my lace, slowly and meticulously tied it in a perfect bow and gave it a tight secure tug with both hands clenched into fists. I rose up out of my seat standing tall, chest pushed out, eyes a little darker and metaphorically grabbed hold of my balls. It was time to go for it.

If I had to make a saying for my approach to being undercover from this point on, it might be something like: 'There's a safety in being bold'. Not stupid bold, but sensible bold. I had to have the mind-set that there was nothing to be scared of. Why should there be? In my mind I was just an infantry recruit who's finally getting to do what they've always wanted to do. People often ask if I was nervous in the Army or scared of being caught. I purposefully took time in the last section to recount how nervous and scared I was on the way in to the Army so you know I'm only human. It's difficult to explain my feelings once I actually arrived there, but from this point on I just wasn't nervous or scared at all. It may sound like I'm trying to be 'macho', but I'm not, I just wasn't nervous or scared anymore. I suppose I couldn't afford to be. If I looked nervous or out of place and I wasn't natural, people would start to suspect something was wrong. My regard for my own well-being must have been my own psychological defence mechanism to override nerves and just get on with it. Perhaps it was also that the anticipation of something is often much worse than the reality of it.

Awareness of our physiological responses and being able to critically reflect on these and know when emotions are useful and to go with them and when to over-ride them with other thoughts is a key element of being resilient. We need lots of opportunity and modelling and practice to be able to do this successfully.

BEING OPEN TO DIFFERENCE

Being open to difference can help us be resilient by learning other cultures and ways of thinking and being. It increases our tolerance for others, while opening us up to experiences where we may widen our perspective on life. Being too inflexible in our thought and assuming things have to only be one way can lead to us not being adaptable or developing our range of ideas and strategies about managing life.

Once I arrived in the Army, I remember almost being surprised at the level of 'normality' and there were a lot of the other guys there in the same boat and being friendly. I suppose I expected everyone to be some 'hardened brute' and somehow substantially different from the 'outside world'. I quickly realised I was just among a group of fellow humans going through a similar experience in life. I was open to a different way of thinking and being and this was something that helped me adapt to and understand the environment I was in, with a range of people.

Others in the platoon I was designated to, had to be open to difference as well as many of them had no experience of further education and seemed shocked that

I had a university degree. On immediate arrival in my new block all four corporals in my platoon had their say about my psychology degree! These ranged from being pleased about it, to trying to persuade me to be an officer, to not understanding why I wanted to be there, to being called a 'government experiment'! I didn't feel different and didn't want to be different because of this. This must have been conveyed in my calm replies as eventually, despite threats of being moved to officer training, the corporals moved on. I think this was also supported with me not appearing condescending to others and having a good physical ability which went against the stereotype of an 'academic'. It was interesting that this undergraduate degree was given an almost mythical status in this context, when in reality it was practically useless for the particular skills and intelligence needed for the Army training experience I was about to embark on. My first report said I was one of the fittest in the platoon and with my competitive drive I was happy with this. It's amusing to me that some are impressed by physical ability, some by academic ability. Some sneer at the opposite ability to which they perceive themselves to be good at. I don't like putting these abilities in binary opposition and I see both areas as valuable to pursue development in to increase your overall resilience, as well as other abilities such as creativity, organisation, problem solving and social and emotional skills. In training I tried to push myself in all areas to make staff want me to stay there and for my own growth.

The other recruits had also started to hear all this talk and asked me about my degree. Most of them weren't bothered really and didn't ask too many questions, but I could see some were surprised and wary at first, mostly because they hadn't been to university. A couple of the lads started to call me 'psycho' because of my psychology degree! It was funny, but I thought it would give the wrong impression to those who didn't know my background and I was keen to discourage that name. It never caught on properly as I didn't really respond or react to it. In the end having a degree actually worked in my favour. Many other recruits seemed comfortable to let me help them with things like bank forms, application forms, quizzes and reading complicated letters amongst other similar tasks. When this happened it was easy to get talking and helped my job finding out if bullying was taking place. I was pleased that many felt able to approach me. I felt some responsibility to try and help the others in my platoon be the best they could be to counterbalance any potential disruption caused to their training if the truth came out about who I was.

I was now Private Sharp and had a number: 30037286. I had been designated to one of many training platoons in the Kings regiment. I will refer to my platoon as 'K' from now on. We were housed in a red brick block near the top end of Vimy Barracks in Catterick Garrison. The end of a cul-de-sac road was just outside the front of our block and it would become our regular place for being on parade and starting and finishing tasks. On the other side of this cul-de-sac from our block was the edge of the assault course and general woodland training area. It was approaching winter time and the trees had few leaves and the ground was muddy and wet. The main corridors of our block had grey rubber flooring on two levels, with the platoon staffs' office and quarters at the top. There were three dormitories on the top floor and three on the bottom floor. I was told I was in 'section 3' of the platoon and given a bed space in a room on the bottom floor. We were given civilian lockers to start unpacking what little of our own stuff we had. We all had another two cupboards for military kit. The room I was given was cold, old and very dusty. We would be cleaning it all up in no time though as a first team building task! My first thoughts on getting a room were for camera angles, security and personal space. My room slept six people and wasn't like the traditional open plan dormitories I was expecting. The room was basically a long corridor in the middle with six alcoves going off for bed spaces. This meant it would be hard to film if anything bad was happening in my room in another space. It was positive that it meant a feeling of having your own privacy. This was convenient for me to fiddle about in my locker without prying eyes. The rest of my bed space had a window, a single metal bed with worn plastic mattress and a shelf or two. The walls were white, marked and dinted. It turned out we could use our phones in the block and were allowed to keep them as long as we didn't use them during the time we were training. It was seen as a morale booster to have phones in the block so recruits could speak to family and friends and keep spirits high during the difficult training. This benefitted me as it meant I could text and speak to the production team fairly freely, especially in the evenings. The reception in my room was terrible though and I had to leave my phone propped up against the window to send a text. I went scouting for the best place to record 30 second video messages that I could send out to the production team as my testimonial evidence. Some of these video messages were included in the BBC programme. It had been suggested that I could record these sorts of messages from the toilets while doing such things like leaving a tap turned on to drown out noise. Each dormitory room had an allocated bathroom with three toilets, a urinal, two sinks and a shower. I tried my first message from a toilet cubicle. I didn't feel safe doing it. The entry to the toilet was an open door that was next to the entrance to the dormitory. People were regularly walking past and could hear. Worse, I had no indication as to when they were coming as the rubber floors made footsteps quiet. The block was usually quiet and the toilet room echoed. I recorded and sent the first message just detailing my first day, but got a feeling like I needed to look for somewhere else. Opposite the toilet was a cleaning room that every dormitory also had. This room had a big heavy door that naturally slammed shut if you let it go. Inside was a few shelves, a large draining area for clothes, a large sink and a little cupboard we put cleaning products in. This cupboard felt much safer. The room had a thick door with a small window and the cleaning cupboard was out of view and earshot of any passer-by. If anyone did open the door it was sticky, noisy and hard to burst through quickly. This would give me enough warning if anyone stumbled upon me filming to quickly put my phone away and walk out the cleaning cupboard with a dustpan and brush. You do so much cleaning in Army training that it wouldn't look unusual for me to always be in and out of this room. This room and cupboard was perfect. It became my undercover sanctuary.

***

I wanted to really immerse myself in Army life to try and understand the culture as best as possible. I thought I could understand what goes on in more depth if I lived it as fully as possible and reflected on how it made me think and feel. I tried to be 'me' as much as possible and go through the experience as naturally as I could, while remaining open to anything that crossed Army guidelines on bullying. This approach was also legally sound as I wasn't provoking anything, merely reacting to it if something happened.

The self maintenance and regimental nature of the Army meant we had lessons in how to shave, clean, iron, make our beds and so on. There was no point in having a chip on your shoulder about being taught these things as everyone picked up something new and there was a specific way these things had to be done in the Army for good reasons. For instance, equipment we ate off in the field had to be very clean to avoid illness from bacteria. A few times my platoon sergeant asked me in a testing way if I thought I was too old for cleaning and being told how to iron etc. The answer I had to give was obvious, but I also genuinely felt I wasn't too old to learn or do things how they were required to be done in this environment. Even the most experienced of us can acquire bad habits in cleaning!

I would say my section was fairly typical, considering the demographic spread for basic training at Catterick at the time. The majority in my section were 18-22 year old white males from the north of England who had qualifications ranging from a couple of GCSEs to an A-level. There were a few older males in their mid-twenties. There was a 17 year old white male from Wales, a 20 year old well educated black male from the Gambia and a 20 year old black male from Ghana. We all got to play football on the first weekend we spent there, which was great for getting to know each other and building morale. Most of the recruits had joined because they always wanted to, some because their family wanted them to, and some because they felt they had little other job options available to them. The Army does provide quite a few options for travel, sports and qualifications that may not be easily accessible to people from certain backgrounds with certain inequality.

Being in the infantry we weren't told that much of the wider context and of large scale Army plans - our job was just to follow orders! However, in terms of being open to difference, it was encouraging that we had specific lessons around Army's values and broader life topics with the Padre and Platoon Commander. These included lessons on politics and on racism amongst other topics. In one lesson a large majority of recruits said they supported the BNP (I later found in November 2010 that the BNP had used a clip of me stating this fact in the Undercover Soldier programme for self-promotion on-line via YouTube before it was taken down by the BBC at my request). There were complex issues surrounding racism in the Army. There were a few people of African origin in our platoon. It was great in the first few weeks to see them sat mixed with all the other young men in the dinner hall. It was also good to see conversations happening in the block about what it was like in their home country in a way that was educational and people genuinely wanted to find out these things. Unfortunately, this didn't last too long. On early visits to the dinner hall, it was very noticeable that among a sea of white faces, there were three tables in the middle that had only black people sat there. It felt like some huge segregation was enforced here, but this wasn't the case. These three tables remained a mystery to me for a while as the black people in my platoon were mixed and sat among us. As the weeks went on I could see how some black and white relations started to separate. A few racist mumblings occurred among some groups of white lads telling jokes about black people and using certain taboo nicknames for them. This wouldn't be to their face, but didn't make the racism any less potent and destructive. Cracks in race relations started to appear over things like music volume, attitudes to mistakes and some language barriers over specific slang. The black people in our platoon edged closer to those three tables in the dinner hall, until eventually they sat on it. People said they were separating themselves, but I realised with these cracks appearing, it may feel more comfortable to sit with people who understand how you are feeling and facing similar issues. I think the three tables came about due to a few cultural differences, lack of understanding and tolerance of these differences and a majority population of young white males from poor northern backgrounds. I spoke with two lads from Ghana and Gambia while secretly filming their stories of being hit by certain corporals. It was never clear cut if these incidents were totally motivated by other reasons or if there was a racial element to them.

Among recruits, the above two races in the Army seemed to almost stand next to each other when it came to racial prejudice against another select group. We became desensitised to certain words that were in the daily lexicon of many, such as 'Ragheads' and 'Pakis'. There were very few people of Middle Eastern descent in British Army training. I heard these words used by all ranks among the main training staff and recruits. It was common place and was also used to describe the enemy in battle training and drills. It's no wonder one lad was caught saying it during a part of training known as bayonet fighting that was filmed for a video available for recruits and their families to buy. He was caught running up to and stabbing a dummy while screaming 'die- fucking Paki'. Many people who saw the Undercover Solider programme said this was the moment that they were most shocked by. I think the reason it's so shocking is the potential it has for breeding hatred, resulting in innocent people being killed in countries at war as well as creating an unhelpful attitude toward others in modern multicultural British society. Prince Harry was even in the news in January 2009 for being caught using the P-word on camera in a military environment. I felt the majority of times the words were used in the Army were for what may be regarded as a 'joke', or to refer to the enemy. Both potentially desensitise a generation to the word and breed an innate hatred of anyone who may be able to be linked to the word, which contributes to difficult societal issues in modern Britain.

I learned there are a lot of mistruths about typical squaddie stereotypes. While I won't deny that there were alcohol and testosterone fuelled moments where behaviours could be similar to that stereotype, the vast majority of training soldiers I met were pleasant human beings who were easy to get on with. There were no crazy initiation ceremonies that people hear about in the rumour mill.

Apart from a few female canteen staff who were slightly older, of a slightly larger frame and had almost as much muscle as the male soldiers, there were no women at Vimy Barracks! This had a significant effect in fuelling female based talk, sexual or otherwise. It meant there was a market for significant sales of pornography, but it also meant there was positive talk of girlfriends and closeness as a motivator to keep going when it got difficult. It meant young male recruits left on a weekend looking to pick up girls in bars, but it also meant many proposed to their girlfriends or made serious commitments as the attachment to that person meant more than it normally did.

The corporals pushed us very hard in the first weeks in terms of timings and expectations of the tasks we did. They were also effectively looking after us 24/7 and became like surrogate fathers in charge of what we did, when we ate, our health, our training, our concerns and our housing. They were the hand that was feeding us and they had been through what we were doing. Due to this there was an automatic respect for them. It was exactly what a lot of the younger members of the platoon needed who craved some stability coming from broken homes. Interactions with the corporals went beyond just training as we lived together, so we started to get to know them and appreciate positive aspects of their personalities. It was a tough job for them in the first six weeks also. I empathised with their position as teachers and role models and tried to understand the pressure of their role for them.

There was a lot of difference in the platoon, but once we started to share time and experiences together these were overcome and we started to pull together. The same can be reflected in everyday life if we take time to seek understanding of others and see them as humans going through the same life experience.

INTER-DEPENDENCE AND GROUP CO-OPERATION

I found the military discipline and their reward and punishment system interesting. It was mostly based on the concept of negative reinforcement, i.e. if you do something wrong, you are punished so you don't do it again. The psychology behind it follows a very behaviouristic practice. I was told there were certain punishments that were used for this negative reinforcement. This was a set of physical punishments such as push-ups, sit-ups, star jumps, running or crawling to who knows where and back, or any mix of the above. Maintaining physical stress positions that were uncomfortable were also used. It was very quickly disheartening and discomforting for anyone doing these. They were not supposed to be used in excess, but as a 'short, sharp shock'. The discomfort usually swiftly went away as soon as you stopped doing the physical punishment, but it was definitely enough so that it deterred you from doing anything that might warrant them. The first six weeks is designed to break down recruits to be later built back up in the way the Army desires. You are deliberately given nigh on impossible timings to get to places and get changed, so when you inevitably fail you learn to respond to discipline and be prepared. The learning curve is extreme and the corporals deliberately distance themselves from being too friendly with you until you have 'learned the hard way' what it takes to be a combat infantryman.

This is different from other settings such as schools that may focus on positive reinforcement and noticing the good things people do to reinforce that behaviour. Positive reinforcement was sparse in the army, but did exist. When it came, it meant something. A word of encouragement went a long way and extra free time (a game of football or even early dinner) were rewards to us. In this environment, for this purpose, physical punishments and negative reinforcement worked as a method of making sure we would do the 'right' thing when it needed to be done. Group punishments were also often used in the early days. This is often something that is frowned upon in both the Army and in other settings like schools. However, I was surprised when I took a long term view of how effective these early group punishments were for building our overall long-term group unity. At first some of these group punishments seemed a bit perverse. For instance, on occasions when we were told to be out at a certain time, those who were out late were told stand still and watch while those out early did the punishments. If someone was doing drills wrong, we all got punished. It was inevitable that those in the platoon who were naturally less able started to be out late or not do drills as well. As you may expect, many in the group started to get annoyed with these people as it felt like we got punished for their mistakes. This initially made those less naturally able members feel uncomfortable and inferior and created animosity towards them. If we had stopped here it would have been ineffective through creating unresolved group tension and discomfort for those who were commonly seen as instigating the group punishment. However, over time there was a realisation (supported by the corporals) that instead of the stronger members getting ready and waiting outside for ages, if we went and helped the less able members in that time we could all get outside together. There was also a realisation that sometimes even the more able members would mess up, causing everyone to receive the punishments. Everyone makes a mistake, forgets a piece of kit, or was last out at some point in time. This led to people checking on each other and helping all around to get ready in time as a group or to complete a task efficiently. If we shared responsibility and supported each other then no-one would get punished or blamed. It got to the point where we would remind each other of difficult parts in drills and help each other practice. We would also go round each other's rooms and make sure everyone else had everything ready for training or any inspections. We ended up helping each other and pulling everyone's ability up. The corporals stopped the group punishments, but everyone continued to help each other out anyway. Whatever you think about the start of this journey into group co-operation from its raw and behaviouristic beginning, we had arrived at a place where we supported each other because we saw a benefit to it, valued it and it made us feel good. Over time the support for each other was not about avoiding group punishment, but about a self-reinforcing, mutually beneficial belief that it felt a good way to be as a human and as part of a group. We all need help sometimes, and helping others not only feels good, but gives us a network of those who can reciprocate. I believe this example tells us something about functioning best as a group when we realise our inter-dependence not only to survive, but to flourish together as well. I'm open to any strategies that help us reach this way of being and have considered applying some of this thinking to interventions in schools that may start with a focus on extrinsic motivation but over time, with careful management and supervision, support intrinsic motivation to build group identity and co-operation.

I think it is natural to us to support each other and we have an instinct to be compassionate[7]. Systems such as capitalism can distract us into being self-focussed, but we have developed as a species over time, across the globe, because we have historically relied on each other to function best as a group. In the Army, you need each other to fulfil different roles and rely on each other to survive. Functioning as a whole is the most efficient way to maintain life. The same is true taking the broad picture of our human existence. We rely on others all the time to be resilient in our day to day life in some form, whether it's directly in person or indirectly though things we have learned previously from others.

Group co-operation also relies on developing a shared language. We had to get used to a whole new set of terminology in Army training. I'm not just talking about all the tactical language or parts of weapons, I'm talking about the daily slang that everyone ends up using. You can recognise someone in the Army just by the things they say. Words like 'civvie' (person who isn't in the army), 'scoff' (food), and 'crow' (new recruit) were all exclusively used within the Army context, along with various politically incorrect phrases for people making mistakes.'

These words became part of everyday language and influenced how we thought and communicated as a group. Every group forms its own slang and whether eloquent or politically correct or not, this slang has a purpose. Slang is dialect created to differentiate groups or tribes and has evolved to associate you with a certain group, whether large or small. It suggests that you have special

---

7 *Keltner, D., Marsh, J., & Smith, J. A. (2010). The compassionate instinct: The science of human goodness. New York: W.W. Norton & Co.*

knowledge not shared by a larger group and confirms your group identity. It strengthens bonds and a sense of belonging because you understand the specific language the group uses.

As well as specific lessons including orienteering, field-craft, battle tactics, chemical biological and radioactive warfare survival and communications, a lot of the first six weeks was spent learning how to march properly. This is one of the most visual displays of group unity I can imagine. We had to be able to do a demonstration march for high ranking officers in order to complete the first six weeks and 'pass off the square'. This earned us a long weekend and the right to wear berets instead of 'crow' caps. If a recruit had a beret on, you knew they at least had some basic skills and knowledge. You looked up to those a few weeks ahead of you in training because you knew they had made it through difficult experiences you were going to have to face. Marching drill was as you may typically expect it to be from films. The sergeant would scream and bark at you if you messed up your steps. It was the only time he would really raise his voice, but when he did, you heard him! There were a lot of steps and techniques to remember and get right. It did take a while and a lot of hours marching up and down the drill square. We got there slowly and surely with repetition. I'm pretty sure I can still remember the marching commands and steps now as it gets drilled into your head that much. I guess that's why they call it drill! Although marching was more of a ceremonial thing, when we were all marching together it did feel like we were 'soldiers'. Marching as a platoon gave you a sense of group identity and being in tune with each other. One quirk about it is that you end up walking 'in step' with all your other friends (in the army or outside) when you are normally walking along the street. I found during my time in training that even when I could have a weekend off, or we left camp to go to a local shop, we would automatically walk at the same pace, with the same foot going to the ground at the same time. My arms would even swing a bit more than they would if I was just walking normally.

Working collectively and group identity can permeate your very being at its most effective and is something that has been essential to our evolution as a species.

MANAGING DEATH AND OUR OWN MORTALITY

Death is something we all have in common. Making sense of our finite lives is one of the core parts of our battle for resilience.

Weapons are designed to kill. I guess it wouldn't be Army training unless weapons, bullets and shooting were involved somewhere! No-one was going to put live bullets and loaded weapons into the hands of any recruit without them learning several handling drills and the theory first! A lot of initial lessons involved us learning what various parts of weapons were called, how to dismantle them, put them back together, and what to do with them when different commands were called out by your corporal. For this we would split down into sections of approximately eight men. Corporals would go through several different lessons with us and we took it in turns to answer, often repeating information over and over again about weapon capabilities and usage. Repetition was a key method of learning in the Army. The main weapon we used was a light assault rifle known as the LA85A2. We were also given a particular number that related to a particular rifle that would become our sleeping partner, life-line, best friend and we would know inside out by the end of training! To practice our shooting initially we had the use of an amazing simulator. It was a wall sized screen and a real rifle that gave kick back and acted just like the real thing. Various aiming programmes and video sequences of 'real life' situations were available to use and all your scores and accuracy statistics were recorded to inform you what you were doing well at and what you needed to improve on. The art of shooting astounded me at first. I had never done any before I started the Army and I learned how so many factors counted in determining your accuracy including the position of your arms and legs, the wind speed and direction, the way you pull the trigger and even your breathing. We only had blank bullets on training exercises for obvious reasons. Some mistakes you can only make once in the real job and if you're not dead, you may have to live with a haunting mistake for the rest of your life. Negligent Discharge or an 'ND' for short, is a cardinal sin in training or at any time in the Army. This is basically when you fire a round from your weapon without being ordered to. It can occur if people are not aware that a round is in the chamber of the rifle, or if they don't keep their safety catch on when they are walking around and press the trigger by mistake. When this happened in training the punishment was severe. A lot of painful running occurred and some people got fined. There were certain recruits who it would happen to more than others and this was a source of frustration for many people. It was a frustration for the corporals as they didn't know if the recruit had really understood the drills or if they were just incompetent. It was frustrating for recruits as drills would break down and we would feel unsafe being next to people who had had a few NDs when we used live rounds. Mistakes with live rounds didn't bare thinking about in training. The first time we used live rounds I was tense. I tried to concentrate hard on my drills but was a bit overwhelmed with the power I had, thinking I could easily kill anyone near me. It seems obvious, but it's a unique moment the first time you have that power at your disposal. Everyone knew the dangers though and listened closely to instructions. We had drills that meant our rifles were always pointing down the range and never turned to face anyone else. We wore ear defenders when firing live rounds as there is a significant volume and kick back difference from firing blanks and live rounds. You quickly get desensitised to firing live rounds after progressing through training. When you near the end of training you let live rounds go at targets without even blinking from all positions such as standing, kneeling, laying down and even walking or running right next to each other.

The weapons we used and bullets we fired were designed for one reason- to kill. The first time the reality of the job was really brought home to me was when we attended a November 11th remembrance service. To attend this service as part of the Army, on an Army base with people who have lost good friends at war, was to have a reminder of the worst side of the job smack you in the face. Death was the air and everyone was inhaling it. This death however was hidden in aching black-holes in everyone's hearts while faces showed passive smiles of 'oh well, that's the job' and lips told darkly humorous jokes of blood, bullets and bereavement. The British Army is renowned for its black humour. I guess in the face of the worst, one coping mechanism is to make light of it. As the pastor was reading out names of people who had died in the last year, I looked around at the sea of perfectly ironed green uniforms. Everyone there was willing to do this job knowing their name may well be read out on that list the following year. I felt like a huge fraud at that point knowing I wouldn't be putting myself in that danger. I hoped that the project would be worthwhile to improve the Army as at this point it felt hideous to pretend to train, knowing I wouldn't have to face the real job like the rest of the people there. My own mortality was brought to the front of my mind and the fact that one day I would die, even if not at war. I found it strangely soothing. Soothing in a way that made me appreciate I was alive now. Managing the sometimes unconscious fear of death is an important psychological process we all deal with through investing in cultural frameworks for living that feel meaningful to us and promote our self-esteem if we live in accordance with them[8]. Our mortality can be taboo to talk about, but I think having a positive shared framework for easing this underlying anxiety can help us live more resilient lives. I hoped others at the remembrance service were having similar thoughts to me, although I think many of us had thoughts of embarrassment and hilarity at how badly we were singing the hymns!

---

8 Solomon, Sheldon, Jeff Greenberg, and Thomas Pyszczynski. 1991. A terror management theory of social behavior: The psychological functions of self-esteem and cultural worldviews. In Advances in experimental social psychology. Vol. 24. Edited by M. P. Zanna, 93–159. Orlando, FL: Academic Press.

Religions based on supernatural beings are an obvious example of a framework for life and death that people have historically used. I appreciate anthropologically how religion has been necessary in helping us make meaning of our lives and can still seem positive in certain contexts. But in the modern world I feel it is a source of segregation and too open to interpretations that have potential to lead to significant human suffering and oppression. I believe the majority of people will find greater and more long-term benefits to human psychological development, resilience and agency from non-supernatural belief. I don't call myself an atheist as it is fraught with philosophical and semantic issues that lead to cyclical debates (i.e. proof of existence) and it means there is not an explicit framework for positively living life. A framework that exists that and I have found is similar to a way of thinking I arrived at independently could be called humanism[9]. This has no need for supernatural belief. This way of thinking resonates with my feeling that while I'm alive, I am blessed to be aware and able to act in the beautiful world and universe. I may be insignificant compared to the magnitude of space, but I am so fortunate to be a small conscious part of it that is able to appreciate it. To help me cope with the thought that one day my physical form will stop functioning, I believe an element of me will continue to exist in the memory of those I have met and interacted with while I was alive. For anyone who knows me, right now they have a conception of what 'Russell' is from their experiences with me in the physical form. Even you reading these words will be building a conception of what or who 'Russell' is. I see the physical form of 'Russell' as a

9 *https://humanism.org.uk/*

vessel for the metaphysical 'Russell', that is the collection of people's memories of interactions with me directly or indirectly. Both are significant, but I see the 'Russell' that is the collection of people's ideas and memories of me as more important than my physical stature. It means that while I'm alive I have the unique opportunity to let my physical form have some impact on how I want people to remember me and shape what 'Russell' is. As I want memories of me to be positive, it pushes me to do positive things while I'm alive and be kind to others. It makes family and children important and supporting those around us. We are inter-dependent in life and by this way of thinking we are also inter-dependent in death, as it is through others that we live on and are connected to through time. This helps us create a sense of meaning within natural human life, placing the emphasis on pulling together as a species and on our positive actions as humans in the physical world. It gives us an ethical code that feels natural and a reason to be good to each other, not one that is given by some mythical being. It puts the locus of control with us as humans and not with some supernatural being who controls what we do. There is no need to focus on some idea of an afterlife that will either scare us into behaving a certain way to avoid punishment or fool us into behaving a certain way for some idea of reward. These can again lead to distancing of ourselves from our actions and has the potential to make people oppress or harm others. A humanist framework for life provokes the type of motivation that helps us make the most of what we have, while bringing us together.

An aphorism I heard many times in the Army was "There is no such thing as an atheist in a fox hole". When we are facing immediate death, any glimmer of hope is needed psychologically to help ease our fear, so there may be some truth in this. I feel this says more about our psychological make up and need for hope, rather than the existence of anything supernatural. Hope can be found in other ways and indeed hope based on 'love' and 'the future' may mean that your desperate last actions to survive may just be the thing that saves you if a grenade is thrown into a hole you are in (as I found out later in training).

If we never think about death and our mortality, it gives us no drive to find positive meaning in our actions in life. If we have gentle reminders of it (as the majority of us naturally do) it allows us to find a good balance between enjoying our desire to live and a bit of helpful cognitive dissonance that keeps us on a path to creating positive connections with ourselves and others.

3:

LOCATING THE ENEMY

"Be Kind, for everyone you meet
is fighting a hard battle"

- *Plato, Philosopher.*

LANGUAGE WE USE AND ITS EFFECTS

The language we use shapes how we understand the world and how we think. It affects how we attribute behaviour and behavioural intentions of an individual. This in turn can affect how we talk about and interact with them, which can cyclically affect how they feel and behave back to us.

The Sapir-Whorf Hypothesis states that there are certain thoughts of an individual in one language that cannot be understood by those who live in another language[10]. It suggests that the way people think is strongly affected by their native languages.

This has implications for how we understand resilience and is important to bear in mind when exploring the concept of bullying.

I haven't mentioned much so far in relation to any signs of bullying I had heard about or witnessed. The BBC programme covers most of the evidential side of the investigation and it is not my intention to revisit everything that was put forward in it or highlight anything new. For the same reason I have also chosen not to use names to re-identify anyone. In week four we had a 'family day' where loved ones were invited onto camp to see where we live and what we do. It's designed to boost morale too. My lovely girlfriend 'Susan' came to visit me! She filmed some drills, my platoon marching and my room that made it into the BBC programme. It was helpful that my platoon staff had seen my 'girlfriend' as this made everything much more real when she was mentioned for any reason. It all felt very normal and because it was the first friendly face I had

10 *Kennison, Shelia (2013). Introduction to language development. Los Angeles: Sage.*

seen in a month it was genuinely great to show someone what I was doing and where I was living. We were all allowed an evening outside of camp, so we went to a local bed & breakfast to do what all boyfriends and girlfriends do when they haven't seen each other for a month! Yep, that's right; talk about evidence of bullying occurring and film myself talking about my experiences in training! I genuinely believe that if I had heard absolutely nothing relating to bullying at this point, the production team may well have pulled me out of the investigation. I had nothing solid and couldn't guarantee at that stage what I may find, but events in certain platoons meant there was some cause for concern.

You can spot the enemy by un-natural shapes in the landscape. Soldiers aim to successfully camouflage themselves against woodland and shrubs. To me the concept of bullying became harder to define the more I thought about it. It didn't always have a clear shape. The concept of bullying can be malleable and constructed in different ways depending on people's world views, context, experience and motives. Bullying can be physical, verbal or psychological, the latter of which can be harder to identify. The views of a perceived victim, a witness and a perceived bully can be subjective depending on the perspective you take and how actions are interpreted. Labelling someone as a 'bully' or a 'victim' can have a psychological impact on them and affect how people perceive them. People may 'bully' others while trying to meet their own emotional needs around esteem or control. There are real psychological effects of being bullied that can have a long lasting impact on a person's mental health. Having a critical stance and a compassionate view to understanding how all in a situation are feeling can perhaps be a way to rebuild relationships and go towards supporting the underlying psychological needs a person has to increase their overall resilience.

Semantics can be an issue here; to which do you attribute the greater force or strength of impact?

A child hit me

My friend hit me

My dad hit me

My office manager hit me

My Army corporal hit me

Written like that, I think the majority of people attribute the hit of the greatest strength or menace automatically to the corporal. Assumptions about the severity of the 'hit' may differ depending on the personal nature, cultural background and historical experiences in the world of the reader. In theory, all scenarios could be of equal strength. It may even be that the child or friend produced the greatest impact. We don't know about the intention of any. It may be easier to assume a 'friend' may not be menacing and a 'child' may be playful. There may be an added shock to the last two scenarios due to them being in a workplace. It may not be shocking that someone who is trained to fight might have hit someone. The 'dad' could have been hitting with the intention of discipline or of abuse. The point is that it impossible to assess the comments accurately and make fair interpretation around what may be 'bullying' without additional knowledge of the context. Context is important.

I personally felt some things I saw first-hand or heard about weren't bullying, some things I really couldn't decide if they were or they weren't (grey areas) and some things that I felt clearly were. In the Army I was watching out for recruit on recruit bullying, corporal to recruit bullying, or other bullying anywhere in the chain of command in any direction. It turned out that the vast majority of what I saw and heard about was in the realm of corporal to recruit bullying. This meant the concept of what might be and might not be bullying was further blurred by commonly held notions in both the public and the Army that it's a 'tough job' and recruits need to be handled roughly in order to prepare them. This further blurs when you consider that some corporals may think they are genuinely trying to 'help' the person by beating them (which may be a view formed from their own background). Despite the complex philosophical, psychological, cultural and ethical issues of where I felt the 'line' was in particular instances relating to bullying, it wasn't really up to me to decide. My job was made simple for me. I was given the Army's own guidelines on bullying and I was told to apply these to what I saw and not to try to impose our own views on what was or wasn't bullying. Some events were fairly clear cut to most people in either organisation and they both had an aim to preventing bullying occurring. No-one would promote the regular beating of a recruit in a toilet. It was the grey areas that were more challenging - such as recruits being pushed over in the field or given a dig in the ribs whilst the corporal was smiling. These had scope to be construed differently by different people without fair context. I decided that I would do the job I had accepted and report everything I saw or heard that broke Army guidelines on bullying, but that I would also make my personal feelings about what I saw or heard in context clear. Despite whatever else happened in the process and how anyone else construed events, I would put faith that the public and/or a court of law would come to fair conclusions about what had happened and that they would probably be similar conclusions to my own. I hoped the outcomes of any court case might inform further practice to improve the lives of young soldiers.

As language and context are so important in understanding people and the world, to help us be resilient and promote harmonious relationships, it is essential to be aware of this and be critical in how we reflect on what we say and hear and how it affects ourselves and others.

KINDNESS

If we are not empathetic in the way we try and understand other's behaviour, we risk misinterpreting feelings, intentions and events. It can be tough to empathise with someone who is threatening you or has spoken negatively towards you, but for our own strength and resilience it is important to try.

If you can't directly see an enemy in the field because something is blocking your line of sight, you might notice them from the shadows they cast on the ground. A soldier needs to be aware of these little signs that could identify something that is hidden from view. As an undercover operative I needed to be aware of small signs that might suggest bullying was taking place even though I couldn't see it. This book is about the internal conversation we all have with ourselves as we try and manage the range of thoughts and feelings we experience as we go through our life on Earth. This too is hidden from our sight as it takes place our brains. We may not be able to see this directly, but we can see some of the signs and manifestations of this internal dialogue through a person's behaviours. We are all undercover operatives or psychologists in one sense in our daily interactions with others as we wonder what others may be feeling or thinking and why. Everyone is fighting their own relative battle in their brains that may be unseen to us and the best response to this is to be kind.

"Kindness in words creates confidence.

Kindness in thinking creates profoundness.

Kindness in giving creates love".

These are the words of Philosopher, Lao Tzu and for me is a summary of the effects of kindness on ourselves and those around us. I think these are essential ways to be to support our esteem, our positive view of the world and our relationships with fellow humans.

I had heard about an incident involving a corporal punching a recruit in the first week and had heard mumblings that ill treatment of recruits in one of our sister platoons in the Rifles regiment (That I shall refer to as 'R') was a fairly regular occurrence. It was very frustrating at first as there were occasions I walked past them in training and could see them, but I couldn't go and talk to them. They were doing training at the same pace as us, but we were kept very separate. There was a bit of innate rivalry that emerged because of this which prevented us from becoming close as two groups. As an undercover reporter I could see and hear signs that there was something relating to bullying going on in this platoon. As a person seeking to understand the situation, I wondered what was happening in the minds of the corporals and the recruits during these events. Our platoon was pushed hard, but

R platoon seemed to be pushed at times to an extreme that likely didn't constitute productive training. Our own corporals commented that R were 'beasted' too hard. This felt a fair comment to us and we appreciated that in general we weren't pushed over the edge or able to get away too lightly with anything either.

We were once placed together on one of the rifle ranges which were wide open spaces with 400+ metres of grass field and banks of sand at one end with targets on. As training was taking place in winter it was usually grey, windy, cold and drizzling. We had just been made to run down a half mile road with our weapons above our heads and crawl through a small ditch that was very muddy with all the rain. We were lined up on the rifle range and my corporal was checking our kit. At this point I saw one of the corporals in R bang the helmeted heads of two recruits together and kick one of them up the backside. I was able to glance to my right and see the incident about 40 metres away (give or take), but it was too quick and a bit too far away for me to warrant pulling my phone out to film. It crossed my mind, but it wasn't worth the risk. I kept my phone in my top left pocket. I always kept it there so it was easily accessible with my right hand and mostly it wasn't in danger of hitting the floor if we were doing physical punishments. I also kept the phone in a small waterproof bag and kept gloves in the same pocket to act as a cushion. At the same training session I also saw another R Corporal shake a few recruits by the helmet straps. Some with medium vigour, some so violently their limbs were flailing about in the air. This same Corporal shook me while I was on the firing line like he shook a few other people. These actions were supposedly in response to us not holding our rifle straight down the range. He seemed insistent on getting this message to our platoon (who he hadn't met before). Safety with live weapons is of course imperative, but we were used to being shouted at and physically punished already in relation to this and had learned our lesson. On a different day I saw the same Corporal take the helmet off a recruit who was lying down in a shooting position and throw it back down on the recruit in the area of his head. He then grabbed the recruit by the scruff of his neck and roughly handled him while screaming in his face. I was very close to this one and my hand rose to get my phone out my pocket as the kerfuffle started. My corporal was stood right next to me though and I was stood on the firing point and it felt too unsafe for both undercover and safe weapons handling reasons for me to start filming. It was an extreme environment to try and secretly film in and on this occasion I opted to just observe intently. There seemed to be more behind these incidents than meets the eye. The corporal may have claimed (or may have genuinely thought) that these methods were the best to learn about safe weapons handling. If this was the case it may have implications for Army training. It may have been that this corporal had a need to assert his authority and feel a greater level of esteem in certain situations. This corporal was suspended during training and it's hard to know what else may have been happening in his personal life and own background that may have affected his behaviour towards others here.

I had heard about one corporal in R that recruits spoke about as being the most threatening. I happened to sit next to an R recruit while we were in the middle of the big stretch of green fields on the range far enough away from the firing line and the corporals. I felt at low risk of being seen by corporals here and decided to film as I asked the recruit about his experiences of the corporal. The recruit was close, but too far away for me to naturally hold my phone in order to speak to him and film him. I spent some time looking for somewhere to prop the phone up on the floor, but we were in a field! I had some equipment with me such as my webbing (utility belt for carrying ammo, grenades and other kit) that I decided could provide camouflage for my phone from all angles apart from the direction I wanted to film. I decided to go for it. The only person who may see it was the recruit I was speaking to and I felt if he did see it, he may just think I was a bit messy and had left things lying around. I pressed record, placed the phone down and went for it. I looked over at him, lifted off my ear defenders and uttered the words 'mate' in the 'excuse me, we've never met but I would like to speak to you' tone. We had to wear ear defender as the sound of 12 recruits all shooting live ammo is very loud! It made talking difficult as we had to shout in order to make ourselves heard. He told me that the Corporal may be getting demoted for hitting another corporal. Crucially, he also revealed to me that the Corporal had 'beaten him up' on an exercise near a farmhouse. I had to clarify what he meant by 'beaten up' in the simplest tone I could so I didn't sound like I was probing too much. He said he had been kicked and punched. The recruit also told me that he had seen the corporal in the local supermarket with his wife and child and the corporal had told him to 'F**k off C**t'. The conversation was short but revealing and I had to do a lot just to get this. It was at this point the recruit noticed the phone and asked in a surprised tone if we were allowed to have them on the ranges. I said the first thing that came into my head which was 'sometimes', even though we weren't really. Having phones was discouraged in working hours, but the enforcing of this relaxed as we got to be more experienced recruits so it wasn't totally out of place. This piece made the BBC programme, complete with the noticing of my phone moment! It became a key piece of evidence. It wasn't the most covert use of my phone, but it served the purpose and I had to be bold to get any information at all recorded. I decided never to stand my phone up on its own to film again as it looked un-natural. I would only ever use it to film again if it was in my own hands and I had a natural reason for it to be out. I wasn't questioned about having my phone on me again throughout all the other filming I did with it.

There was more to find out about the background of the corporals, the training they had been given and the issues they faced in order to fairly make some conclusions about what was happening around these incidents of aggression. The same is true for understanding any fellow human in our everyday lives. Kindness can help our connections to others and understanding of them. This supports our positive relationships which is essential to our resilience.

LIFE AFFIRMING EXPERIENCES

We all have peak experiences at some point that cultivate a feeling of gratitude and of appreciation for life that allow reflection on the 'bigger picture' about what is important to cherish. These 'wow moments' occur randomly and fleetingly and it's nice to be able to hold on to them or revisit them as often as we can to develop our sense of wellbeing. Out in the field we were taught not to create a silhouette of ourselves against the skyline or in windows of buildings. In the bright flashes of rapid gunfire in a dark stone urban battle zone your silhouette flickers in and out of existence, mirroring our brief moments of extreme joy and how our own life can be there one minute and gone the next. There is nothing like a few days extreme physical activity and training for warfare in a cold, bleak field to breed moments that alter your perspective on what is important in life. I would like to share some of my peak experiences with you.

When training for urban warfare you get to climb up ladders to enter occupied buildings, jump through windows and attach a flashlight to your rifle letting it cut through dark corridors searching for a glint of an enemy. You get to let off pyrotechnic grenades, kick down doors, shout 'clear' at the top of your voice after storming a room and let off a few rounds into likely enemy positions. It sounds just like an action film on paper! It's not all smooth slow motion diving through the air and bullet time movement though. It's real and very physical. Diving through windows really hurts when you land on the concrete floor below! You don't feel the physical damage at first due to the adrenaline, but you always leave urban warfare training with messed up elbows and bleeding knees. During one training session in what was termed the 'ghost house', we were kitted up with electronic tags on our limbs and lasers on the guns so all our movements could be tracked and played back to us on video to work out what we had done right and wrong. A brilliant tool for trainee soldiers and it's a shame we only got to do this once in training as I think the more practice with this the better. I had been put into the first assaulting pair (the lead two to break into the building). We located an open window on the first floor of the enemy house. I leaned a ladder up against the wall and I was first up. Standing on a small ledge under the window I pulled a grenade out to throw inside and clear the room. I noticed a figure on the roof looking at me and I panicked ducking for cover, but it was just one of our corporals taking a photo of me to record the event! I carried on, throwing the grenade through the window and ducking down to wait for the blast. As soon as I heard the grenade go off I dived through the window firing a couple of shots and found a good position to kneel and aim my rifle, before shouting out to my comrades what I could see in the room. I was joined by another member of the team as we both trained our rifles on a door and an open hole in the wall waiting for the next assaulting pair to come through. There was suddenly a noise from the next room. The door opened a crack and a small metal object bounced into the room and stopped in front of us. It was a grenade.

I had never had a grenade thrown at me before, so it took my brain a second to process. I simply stared at it before deciding it was too late to run so my best option was to dive into the corner in a ball and hope I don't get blown up too badly! That sounds stupid and cowardly, but it was the decision I made. If I had more time, was braver or had previously thought about it, I would have run towards the grenade and kicked it back through the door. I also learned to secure doors shut so no-one can drop things through open cracks! In the end, my decision wasn't actually that bad. According to my electronic pack, I didn't die in that blast, I was only injured. My desperate actions and glimmer of hope to cling to life had been enough to save me (I literally was an 'atheist in a foxhole' in this case). I had been far enough away and in enough of a curled up ball to protect my vital organs. The 'grenade' made a tacky fake explosion sound like an old arcade game and an electronic pack on my side vibrated and kindly told me I had been hit. I knew it was only training and no real harm would come to me, but I couldn't help reflect on people who have faced a similar situation for real. I felt I had only got a taste of the fear, confusion and panic. It was only about a second that I stared at the grenade, but it felt like so much longer and I could see how there must be time for your 'whole life to flash before your eyes'. When I curled up thinking that there was nowhere to run, I thought that if this was for real I would be waiting for the pain of an exploding grenade ripping through my body and hoping that I'm in a good enough position to not die! My back that took the impact would have been a burned mess. I would be deaf from the blast and would have stained the floor red as I crawled to the door to help keep it closed for my team. In the simulation I ended up dying from a second grenade thrown by my own platoon who had aimed at the enemy in a corridor on the other side of the door I was propping shut. Although we were a good section and led well, we bungled this attack from inexperience at facing those types of situations. I found contemplating my death was actually life affirming and reminders of our mortality can make us appreciate being alive now.

At the end of the four day urban warfare training, I experienced one of the greatest feelings of physical power and dominance I have ever felt. We trained in a little village with a few derelict buildings that is used by the

Army, the Police and other armed professions as a place to practice 'Fighting In Built Up Areas' (FIBUA). We had slept in one building for two nights and kept watch at all hours as we defended it from random enemy attacks. This was exhausting and the people playing the enemy used devious tricks to surprise us. One dark night, six of us were piled in one upstairs room in the stone building with two others manning a sentry point we had made from putting several sandbags by a small window. As others tried to sleep, I was sat up looking out the window down a long driveway with a building to my left and trees to the right. I kept my eye out for anything moving. About 2am, I saw a vehicle driving slowly up the road towards us. This could have been anyone and not necessarily part of training. However, there was something strange about its speed as it was travelling slowly. My eyes narrowed on my camouflage painted face as I focussed through the night air assessing the vehicle. I looked through the scope on my rifle for a magnified view and I saw four sets of boots walking behind the vehicle. This was a surprise attack and they were using the vehicle for cover. A split second after I realised what was happening, they popped out from behind the vehicle and started firing. I was quick to fire back and shout 'Stand to' at the top of my voice for everyone else in the building to join me in defending ourselves. The whole house awoke and ran into firing positions for a quick response in shooting back. The enemy played dead quickly as they knew they had been caught. We came to think fondly of our little building after sleeping in it and defending it. It's funny what we as humans end up being attached to. We eventually had to practice escaping from it, as if the enemy over powered us and gassed us out. We escaped and spent one night in the field a way away from the area before getting up early the next morning to march back and reclaim our village. This is where my feeling of mankind's power when we're all fighting together came in. We slowly marched in single file towards the village to reclaim it. We got up at 2am to prepare and get there in time for a sunrise attack. My feeling came when we were just arriving back at the village. We were a few hundred metres outside and the sun was just rising giving us a warm energy boost. We had joined with other platoons practicing the same thing and we were 100 men strong with a vengeance for being kicked out 'our' village. It was like the calm before the storm. We looked like a giant four hundred metre long venomous green snake slowly and silently winding along a dusty road, ready to obliterate any foe that was in our path. At this time in our training our muscles were built, we were experienced in tactics and training and knew what we were doing with precision. We were also armed to the teeth with grenades, rifles, machineguns, ammo and equipment for breaking into houses with speed. It just felt like absolutely nothing could f**k with us at that moment. Sorry for the expletive, but that was literally what went through my head. It was one of those feelings that made you grip your rifle a little tighter, stare a little harder, grit your teeth and literally feel the adrenaline rising inside you. There were so many of us and we were trained killing machines. We were going to get our village back and absolutely nothing or nobody was going to stop us. I heard my Section Commander comment it was like marching to Stalingrad. Psychologically, once in that state of mind, there would be no turning back! I reflected how the powerful feeling builds bonds and is motivating, but also how the feeling could make men hungry for more power in a way that is negative to us all.

I also had a feeling of awe in training for the power of man-made machines. When you are fighting on foot you can access anywhere and it's easy to hide, but you can't move quickly and are vulnerable from limited power and resource. If you had just fought a few hours battle, had lost men and you were physically exhausted to the point of almost giving up, it must be the best feeling to see a friendly fighter jet zoom in over your head and obliterate the enemy in a matter of seconds. The RAF had a display day during our time in training and one jet went from being a dot in the sky to right on top of us in a matter of seconds. I thought it was incredible. When I say right on top of us, I mean I could literally see the detail on the underside of the plane. It got as low as maybe 3 or 4 standard houses in height if they were stacked on top of each other. The noise was so loud it literally made people lose their footing and everyone automatically ducked. A few seconds later it was a dot in the sky again. If that had come to attack us, we would be gone before we even realised it. I reflected on our technological achievements as mankind and the sheer power we can control. Just flight itself is amazing as we have overcome our physical limitation, but fighter jets are something else. The addition of electronic systems, radars and weapons means you have something that can end many lives in seconds without being able to be touched. Despite the grave moral and ethical dilemmas of creating weapons and machines that are designed to kill us, it's hard not to slightly marvel at the feat of engineering and the physical power mankind can create that significantly extends our comparatively feeble bodies.

I had peak experiences that were about the beauty of the world in all its natural splendour and being grateful to be part of it in our brief human life. I came to term these feelings 'Simple Joys' after a phrase I heard from a children's summer camp I worked on in 2005 in North Carolina, USA. Some of the harsh physical environments in training made simple things so much more appealing and were a reminder that most of us take things for granted in the modern world. Things such as sleep, food and sunlight provided feelings of immense pleasure after extended periods of physical activity in the cold, muddy, wet night time in the middle of the North Yorkshire moors. It was funny how the same place and activity could produce some of the best and worst moments depending on what the natural world threw at us. For instance, sat on stag duty (watching out for enemies) in training could be peaceful. I would usually go on one of the first duties in early evening then another in early morning when we were out in the field. On one early evening, I sat out in the wonderful country side with the fresh smell of woodland. I saw the sunset before the stars emerged and I had a warm flask of freshly brewed tea and chocolate to keep me company while I sat and admired the view. I laughed to myself that I was getting paid for this and forgot all about being undercover, bullying and even Army training for a while. I went off to sleep with a smile. Fast forward five hours and I'm being given a little kick to wake me up. The weather had changed to torrential rain and half my stuff had got wet because our poncho had leaked. I couldn't see anything in the pitch black and I had to drag myself out of my sleeping bag into the cold and dress in full combat gear and go and sit in a muddy puddle for two hours trying to fight falling asleep. There was no food or drink to keep me awake and there was the threat of a surprise attack. I sat shivering and thinking about how wonderful the exact same spot was just five hours earlier. I reflected that no-where is sacred on earth, it can really depend on the context you are in and what is happening around you that brings you contentment.

We were encouraged to take 'bags of morale' with us on exercise. This was basically a bag of sweets. I never had much of a sweet tooth, but I soon saw how a bag of morale really worked. It's amazing how when sat by yourself, freezing cold in the pouring rain, a little reach into your pocket and a bit of a sugary taste on your tongue makes everything seem, well, fractionally less s**t! Chocolate muffins became my morale from hard days of training or if I was feeling low from being undercover for too long. If I hadn't been doing so much physical activity I would have become fat from all the chocolate muffins of morale I ate to get me through the six months.

Another 'simple joy' occurred one of the first times we had slept outside and it was a bitterly cold night. The training staff had word that it was between -7 and -10 degrees Celsius and so we should cancel training as our bodies weren't used to that temperature yet. We were told to all get into our sleeping bags and try and keep warm. I didn't sleep that much as even in clothes and a sleeping bag you could still feel the cold that night. The following morning we were woken up and they made us go for a gentle jog, just to get the blood flowing and keep us warm. When we got out of our wooded sleeping area and onto the moorland I saw something beautiful. For miles across the moors it was like a white winter wonderland. Snowy fields glistened like a fresh blank canvas that was just about to be painted by the sunrise. A small golden ball rose on the horizon turning the whole sky pink and purple. This was then reflected on the snowy moors and the sight was just incredible. It made the freezing night worth it, just to see this. It really showed me that every cloud has a silver lining. Or pink in this case!

A final peak experience requires me to ask you a question: What is the most satisfying drink you have ever had?

Is it a fine champagne? A fine aged malt whisky? A juicy ice cold Ribena?!

I'll tell you what mine is: a completely cold, sugar filled tea with little bits of grass in.

I was physically and mentally exhausted. I was dehydrated, hadn't slept for a couple of nights and just finished carrying the heaviest member of our platoon two miles across the windy moors. I staggered up a dusty road having finished the gruelling exercise with a dry mouth and body that was depleted of energy. I reached into my webbing, pulled out my flask and poured the most satisfying drink I have ever had over my pursed dry lips. I could literally feel it go down my throat and 'ping' straight away to the areas of my body that most needed nourishment. That drink made me happier than any expensive drink I will ever have in a bar. Bertrand Russell in his book 'The conquest of happiness'[11], speaks of eating simply because you are hungry as a more positive and

11 Russell, B (2013) The Conquest of Happiness 1st Edition: Liveright, New York.

authentic feeling that outweighs chasing the perfectly cooked steak at a world class restaurant. This relates to enjoying the variety of life in every day experiences, rather than seeing them as banal and tedious and seeking only euphoric experiences. The satisfying of a basic human need for survival is a greater feeling of contentment than is possible from chasing anything we have idealised as a modern society and made very expensive. Bertrand Russell suggests those chasing the 'perfect taste' will inevitably feel they are not happy unless they experience an even better taste at an even finer restaurant every time they eat. I understood what he meant in the moment as I drank my wonderful cold sugary grass filled tea and felt wonderful. Experiences like this do change your perspective of what you moan about. It's so easy when working day in and day out in a city that's like a concrete jungle to get your head caught up in the stress of paperwork and corporate responsibility. I still get caught out like that from time to time and find my head looking at the pavement as I walk, rather than the sky. But if I get too low, I usually remember the above experiences and it gives me better perspective of what we should be grateful for and what is actually worth complaining about.

PHYSICAL ACTIVITY AND HEALTH

There are obvious benefits to having a healthy body to help us negotiate the world. Physical health also contributes to our mental health and can help us feel more energised and able to face our day. Regular exercise helps release feel-good brain chemicals that may ease low mood (neurotransmitters, endorphins and endocannabinoids). Regular exercise has many psychological and emotional benefits too and can help you build confidence, take your mind off worries and get some of your own space.

Movement and speed is something that may draw the eye to an enemy. Army training is full of intense physical activity that supports develop your effective movement. Although everyone had to pass certain fitness grades to join the Army, when we started there was a variety of fitness levels. The fitness training programme progressively pushes everyone to their own limits and by the end most people are of a similar fitness level.

There is a real difference between 'fitness' and 'Army fitness'. Army fitness is extremely robust. You can have people who may seem like great athletes, look really strong or run really fast, but dress them in full combat gear with a 60Kg bag on their back and quick march them up a hill and they soon start wanting their mummy. When I joined, I had the same perception a lot of people have, which is that big muscles mean good fitness. I learned this is untrue. We had nick-named one of the recruits in our platoon 'the terminator'. You can imagine the type: over 6 feet in height, muscles that make the t-shirt rip, washboard stomach. The type if you came across in a dark alley you might feel the need to turn and run the other way. They make you have doubts about your own fitness and feel insecure. Well, that is until we actually started to do some fitness. Despite looking as he did, he was without a doubt the weakest member of the platoon fitness wise. He could hardly do any press ups, only a few sit ups and as for running, he would stop after 500m and the rest of us had to pull him along. So next time you see guys who stand around in clubs in tight t-shirts, full of steroids, thinking they look great, I pretty much guarantee their fitness levels will be laughable. You end up with strong natural muscle after Army training, but not necessarily 'built like a brick s**t house'. It is widely suggested that steroid use is increasing in society among young men[12]. This may be for a number of reasons, but being naturally fit and strong is much better for your physical and mental health.

There were two types of physical training in the Army. 'Normal fitness training' : runs, press ups, sit ups, circuits in the gym, and 'Combat fitness training': crawling through mud, carrying logs, tabbing (speed walking with full combat gear on) for miles, carrying each other, assault courses. I learned a lot from combat fitness training and had to go through it in order to progress the investigation. There were times throughout this when I would think, why am I voluntarily doing this? I kept going as I wanted to put myself through what every recruit has to do to really understand the experience.

People often ask me what the physical training in the Army was like, so I would like to share the five hardest moments for me individually. The challenge of these experiences can be relative to the individual, but I would think they would be fairly similar for most in training. Following this, you might understand why many people suddenly decided they had a twinge in their left toe that meant they had to go and see the doctor when it was time for combat fitness! If you want to briefly experience this fitness style, put down the book for a second and lie flat on your front. Without lifting your head or your bum, try dragging your body forward using your arms and knees.

---

12 *http://www.telegraph.co.uk/news/2017/07/27/steroids-see-four-fold-increase-data-shows-fuelled-rise-muscle/*

It may help to bend them at a 90 degree angle like a frog. Go across your room and back. Go on. I'll wait...

That was fairly hard right? Now imagine having to do that over gravel and hills for hundreds of metres regularly. With that in mind here are some stories of what Army physical training was like.

In week four we got 'logged'. This involved running while carrying a log shaped like a tree trunk! We did several log runs over the course of training, but this hurt the most because we were all new and our muscles had not yet adapted to Army fitness. Picture small groups of new recruits with a tree trunk on their shoulders hurriedly staggering along North Yorkshire moorland covered in mud and sweat after already doing about an hour of training and you may start to get an idea. This exercise really shows the people who try and put the effort in and have the competitive drive and those who shirk off. It is also one of those exercises that works for all ability levels equally as the fittest people have to take more weight than those less fit (or less hard working). Everyone came back that day with cuts on their shoulders and bad backs. It did break us in to Army fitness and after we had rested and rebuilt ourselves it did make us stronger - It was just painful at the time. Although I got countless cuts and bruises and aches from training, this was the only point I thought I had actually done some real damage and it was so early on in training. I had really pushed myself and my back hurt for about two weeks after. Simply carrying my dinner tray seemed to put my back in the certain position that caused the most pain. What good is a soldier who can't even carry a dinner tray across the canteen! I guess I was a bit fool hardy to not get it medically checked, but I think I knew I had just strained a muscle and if I didn't aggravate it and kept stretching it then it would be ok. Fortunately the other lessons and fitness we did around that time didn't really involve the back muscles (I think the fitness programme was structured like that on purpose) and I lay on my floor every night in various positions and really stretched my back out. After a week I could feel it getting strong again and subsequent log runs didn't feel so bad.

A loaded march or 'tabbing' is a cornerstone of Army fitness. You work up from doing three miles with hardly any weight, to a quick eight miles carrying what is effectively a small house on your back! If you want to know what it's like, find your nearest hill, pack a bag full of rocks, put your head down and try and walk as fast as you can and see how long it is until you get tired. Then when you do get tired, imagine being shouted at and looking ahead to see you have only gone two hundred metres and still have seven miles, one thousand four hundred metres to go. We got used to tabbing and actually it was great fitness and felt core to the real job where you may have to carry all your equipment across to where it's needed as quickly as possible with only manpower. I found the hardest of all of the tabs we did was one of the six mile ones. The PTI (Physical Training Instructor) was in a grumpy mood and had been short changed at the last minute to take our lesson (which meant he had to do the tab himself too). One of our Corporals said in a joking tone 'you lot are in for it!' Normally, the PTI was chatty to the corporals, but this time he was hardly speaking and marching us straight off. I don't know what time we did the six miles in, but it was quick. We basically ran the whole way even though it was supposed to be a tab. When you run with all that weight on your back, it's more of a jog that gets nicknamed 'the squaddie shuffle'. Six miles of squaddie shuffling up and down the moors is painful! The PTI just kept screaming at us about Helmand province and kept forcing us on. An ambulance followed us round on certain tabs in case people were seriously injured. I can't remember if anyone had to get the ambulance back to camp on this occasion as I was too focussed on my own pain, my own legs, my own breathing and trying to get to the end in one piece. The only silver lining to this experience was that it made the seven mile tab seem pretty easy!

The hardest session when you looked at what we did on paper was a mix of three strenuous activities put together when we usually only did one of them. The steeple chase, the assault course and a log run. This was the final CFT session we had so we were all in peak physical shape and they hit us with everything they had. We had to carry a log all the way around the 1.5 mile steeple chase (rough surfaced running track with water pits to go through), followed by exercises with logs, followed by the whole assault course (consisting of cargo nets, rope swings, walls to climb over, balance beams, nets to crawl under and a few jumps). A new recruit would not have managed this and there were times when if you told us we had to do all that at once, we wouldn't have believed it. As we were in peak shape we did manage to do it and I'm still surprised that I didn't feel so bad after it. I guess it shows the training works.

Bayonet training. Those words cause anxiety when they come into contact with the ears of recruits. This is what warfare stamina and carrying on through anything is about. The corporals deliberately mess you about for a few hours (i.e. give you stupid times to get to places and repeatedly get changed). When you inevitably don't make the timings, the pain starts and the first time we did this it was a crawling extravaganza! We crawled back and forth in a cold pool of water a couple of times while trying to keep our bayonet and rifle dry and clean. We were soaking, freezing and confused, but after this we went around the steeple chase continuing the crawl over gravel and mud (the mud being a blessing as it was so much softer than gravel). This crawl would intermittently be changed for a few hundred metre sprints, which actually came as a bit of a rest from the pain of crawling. We had to just keep going until we were told to stop- there was no goal or clear end point in sight. To cope with this you get into a unique frame of mind that is hard to describe, but I imagined being like a robot that just continues going and doesn't think about any pain or about any end point but just movement in limbo where you may keep going for eternity. It's a frame of mind that you have to get used to if you want to build up your mental stamina and resilience. This state of mind can be applied to everyday difficult situations when you are uncomfortable and you need to keep going. If you think about an end point, it is worse and you can break if you get near to what you believe to be 'the end' and then the goalposts move. An exercise that really developed this way of thinking was simple circuit running, but when we were coming to the 'home straight' we would turn off and keep going, numerous times. It wasn't over until it was over. We had gone about half a mile and we were struggling to crawl any further, but more crawling came. We had to crawl in a big circle up and down a grassy hill until our elbows and knees were grazed - then we got to carry on back on the steeple chase. When we eventually stopped we emerged in an open field I had never seen before. We were made to do more running across the field while the Corporals set up some target dummies that we would imminently be taking our frustrations out on! Before we did, we had to see red. We were made to stand in a big group, muddy from crawling, face streaked in camouflage paint that had run from profuse sweating, knees bloody and all start stamping our feet in rhythm. On top of this we had to keep shouting "Kill, Kill, Kill" at the top of our voices. It was like we were manufacturing the essence of violence, aggression and destruction and managing to contain it all in a platoon shaped jar, ready for someone to unscrew the lid and unleash hell. We were shown the techniques of how to stab an enemy and then instructed to practice. People let out primal screams as they lurched forward and put all their pent up anger and frustration into forcing the steel blade on the end of our rifle as far into the straw dummies as possible. I did it myself, focussing only on inserting death into those dummies and letting my rage out. In the moment it was like I was facing life and death where it would either be me or him who would die- and it wasn't going to be me. It was also a strangely therapeutic way of letting out pent up frustration. After I had had a few goes, I stopped to reflect for a moment and look around. You could literally see the red in people's eyes and what can only be described as a mist of rage floating over us all. We had seemingly totally changed from polite boys who sat at camp and played computer games to raging warriors, intent on death. We did a second bayonet training several weeks later which was technically more demanding, but not quite as painful or as strange experience as doing it for the first time.

The final scenario to give you a taste of physical life in the Army was our first casualty evacuation (Cas Evac). This was done after three nights sleeping out in the field and our first full scale practice battle. In short, we were exhausted to start with. We had just finished and the Corporals dropped two dummy grenades at our feet. As the fuse popped we got shouted at again- It's not over until it's over! We were straight into a drill pretending one of the men in our section was shot and we were under attack again and had to evacuate. Our Corporal decided to test us and picked the biggest recruit in our platoon - a fourteen stone lad, whose weight was around his middle. We tried to grab an arm and a leg each and carry him but his weight just pulled us all together and we kept collapsing. We couldn't even lift him high enough to get him on our shoulders as we were too weary. Despite all of our Corporal's shouts and threats of writing bad reports, we just couldn't keep moving him quickly. One of the lads in our section literally gave up and walked behind us. He got sent back a few weeks in training for this. The rest of us tried to keep going slowly. I saw a white van in the distance about 500 metres away. I thought, that's probably a pretend ambulance, if we get him there we will be ok. We struggled on and on moving him a few metres at a time until we eventually closed in on the white van. We sort of stopped thinking we had done it, but then our Corporal screamed 'What the hell are you doing, we're not stopping here… We're going all the way back to the rendezvous point'. This was another mile away. I stared at the floor in disbelief thinking that it wasn't possible. I usually never have that attitude and like to think I'm very determined to overcome any challenge. On this occasion, I honestly thought at that moment we just physically wouldn't be able to do it, even if we were being shot at for real. We couldn't go on carrying him by his arms and legs so we were allowed to take it in turns to individually give him a fireman's lift and jog about 20m with him before swapping to someone else. This gave you a short rest before your 20m stint again. The weather was also sleeting at this point as we stared down the long winding stone county road in the direction of our objective that we couldn't even see. We just kept going. We managed to get into the frame of mind that we were in a limbo where we just had to go forever and there was no end point. The corporal eventually switched to being verbally positive when we put effort into our 20m run. He could see we were physically at our limits. We didn't really speak and just carried on staring forward like zombies and squeezing every bit of energy out of us. Somehow, we made it back. I have no idea how long it took us, but we did make it. It just goes to show what you can do even when you think you can't. I've never been so physically depleted. As I mentioned, a cold sugary tea with bits of grass in is a highly recommended drink after such an experience to make you feel SO much better!

Having given you these extreme examples, a lot of the physical training was quite enjoyable and you did feel yourself improving. The rate at which they pushed you seemed well planned and you could feel it working well. I know at the end of training I was at the peak fitness I will ever be. Despite being in a complex situation, I was feeling mentally fit, able and resilient too as my whole body was healthy and strong. We can take our fitness and health for granted, but maintaining it and developing it is so important for our overall wellbeing.

GOOD ORGANISATION

Having good organisation of your equipment was also a key learning point in Army training so you could act and move quickly when required. I learned positive ways to organise my possessions and my mind to function efficiently in this environment as a recruit, as an undercover reporter and as a person.

During the early exercises (combat/survival practice) out in the field, the corporals know the rookie mistakes everyone always makes and are sure to jump on them when they happen to make sure you don't do it again. New recruits usually leave some litter. You can give your location away to an enemy if they notice a different texture on the landscape or they catch a glimmer of reflected sunlight from your metal weapons or equipment. This can give the enemy vital information about who they are dealing with. Recruits also usually leave their kit in an untidy, unregimented fashion on their first trip into the field. This makes it easy for an enemy to sneak around and steal weapons. It also means equipment is likely to get left behind in the chaos of a surprise attack or if you have to leave in a hurry. After the first few times of losing kit from the corporals springing a surprise attack, you start to be on edge about where you leave everything and what the corporals might be plotting to trip you up. This can create good habits of organisation so you know where everything is at all times. It can also leave you like a little child sat up in the night, eyes flicking from side to side, trying to work out what the noises are you can hear. One story of my own idiocy of this style occurred when I had just finished one of my stag duties (watching out for enemies while the rest sleep) in the middle of the night and had come back to my sleeping bag and put all my kit in a tidy position around me and got ready to get warm and get some much needed sleep. We were expecting a surprise attack at some point (which sounds ironic but you would never know exactly when they would come) and it made me hyper sensitive to changes in 'normality'. You sleep in your boots and with your rifle so you are ready to jump out the sleeping bag if you are called upon ready for action (and also so no-one can steal your rifle if you are asleep). Something woke me and I did that motion of moving my head to different positions to try and locate the sound as the forest is pitch black in the night. I was running on instinct, but was still half asleep in my thinking as my thought process went a little something like this:

'What was that noise...It was something near me...and it was ticking. What the hell is ticking? A bomb!? It's only training... maybe it's a booby trap left by the corporals that will go off in the surprise attack to come. Hang on, where is my helmet? Uh-oh, I left it a little outside the sleeping area. That ticking, it's echoing like it's in something dome shaped...wait, there's something in my helmet! Maybe it's a new trick by the corporals to put something that goes bang in anything you leave outside your sleeping area to prove a point that the enemy might sneak up on you, or to show that you shouldn't leave your helmet upturned as things may fall in it. No, hang on, maybe it's just an insect stuck inside my helmet...no, it's too mechanical and regular for an insect. It is some clockwork device inside my helmet....I've got to get rid of it...'

So, after all these thoughts, I picked up the helmet hoping I wouldn't set off whatever was inside and thrust it out in-front of me holding the helmet tight so whatever was inside was launched out into the middle of the dark branch infested forest floor and well away from me. Phew! I turned over and got a delectable couple of hours sleep until an actual surprise attack came at the break of dawn and we had to jump up into action and return fire while packing everything away ready to evacuate the area. Chaos, confusion, gunfire and explosions. We escaped the attack and were enjoying a rare break sat with a brew and a biscuit overlooking the North York moors. The guy who I had shared a sleeping area with that night leaned over and said 'Oi Sharp, I think I've lost my watch somewhere'. 'Bummer' I said, while continuing to sip on my tea and wondering what he wanted me to do about it. 'I think I left it in your helmet last night when I went on stag duty' said the recruit. 'Oh right', I replied passively while still enjoying the view and munching on my biscuit. Suddenly my brain processing kicked in and I started laughing and realised that the mini-panic I had had in the night over ticking booby traps was actually just his watch and I had inadvertently thrown it away into the depth of the woods! I managed to rummage round the rough area I knew it must have gone and I found his watch. Not quite the way I was intended to learn this lesson I'm sure, but I never left my helmet outside my sleeping area or upturned again!

I also had to make sure anything I had filmed wasn't seen and that I was able to get it out of camp to give to my production team to start making the BBC programme.

My phone was such a vital piece of equipment, but one that could give me away or make the investigation almost impossible if it broke or got lost. It required good organisation to keep it functional and safe. The first time I thought I may lose the use of my phone as a method of communication as well as a video recorder was in the first week. Someone had lost their phone in our platoon, but at the time they thought it was stolen. When the recruit reported his phone had been stolen the corporals instantly made us all get our phones and keep them in a big metal box in their room as we 'couldn't be trusted'. I had the briefest window to send a text to the production team that literally just said 'phone going'. I didn't have any footage on the phone at this point and all names of production team members were cunningly hidden as Susan, or other friends. This probably panicked the production team for a while and was of concern to me, but deep down I think I knew we would get them back soon enough. We did, the next day.

A close call to someone discovering footage I filmed on the phone came at the hands of one of the recruits I felt a genuine friendship with in training. He had a new phone and was messing about with blue tooth. I had five small SD memory cards of varying memory capacity that could be put in and out of my phone and easily hidden. About half way through training and I had become slightly slack about removing memory cards as I had become a bit too comfortable and no-one seemed to be suspecting anything. Despite that, something nagged me in my brain and I decided to adhere to my system and remove a memory card with about four videos on of a recruit talking about being beaten and seeing people beaten. The moment after I had done that, I got a message from my fellow recruit (who was in the room next door) saying I had to enter a pin code to allow him Bluetooth access. I hadn't used Bluetooth much before and was intrigued to what it did if I put that pin code in. After doing that I walked next door to see what was going on. I was met with my fellow recruit grinning and saying, 'you haven't got s**t on your phone Sharp'. As I dryly smiled back I realised the passcode I had entered had given him remote access to all the files on my phone. I was very thankful I had just switched my memory card to a blank one. The rest of the evening I thought how close I had been to him watching videos I had filmed of fellow recruits talking about bullying that would surely have made him confront me about what I was doing. I breathed a sigh of relief and made a mental note to be as tight as possible with switching memory cards that have evidence on and also to not give anyone blue tooth access to my phone!

On the final exercise I had to do in the Army there were two occasions when I thought my phone was done for and key evidence was lost. The first of these took place on a dark night in the middle of some woods in Scotland. In some of the dense woods it was literally pitch black at night as there was no moon or artificial light anywhere. I remember one night getting woken up, getting ready, packing my stuff and then going to sit down on sentry duty that was a little way away from our sleeping area. I got ready for my two hour shift, sat down on the ground and made myself comfortable. I reached into my top left jacket pocket where I kept my gloves (they provided padding for my phone) and suddenly had a surge of adrenaline and panic. I realised my phone wasn't in the pocket and that my zip was already open, meaning that it had been open when I was walking and my phone had probably fallen out on the dark forest floor in some random ditch of mud. I thought I was in real trouble. The phone had evidence on it and I didn't know how on earth I was going to find it in the pitch black without making a lot of noise or shining a lot of light and alerting someone. I couldn't wait until the morning as we may get attacked and have to move off from the area never to return. The Corporals may also search the area first thing to see if we have made a mess and if they see a phone they will have a field day looking at it. I would be screwed as they would see recordings of me and recruits speaking about them. What occurred next is a testament to the good training I received about organisation and operating in the dark (no innuendo!). We got used to being able to pack and unpack our bags and store our equipment by touch and feel alone with no use of torch light (which could inadvertently signal our position to a watching enemy). I remembered that when I was rolling up my sleeping mat to go on sentry duty there was a sound like something dropped on the floor that didn't make sense at the time and I assumed it was just a bit of wood or something from the forest. Something triggered in my brain that gave me a vague hope that the irregular sound I heard might have been my phone falling. I wasn't sure, but thought the best place to try find it was back at my sleeping area anyway because if it wasn't there I was never going to find it in the rest of the dense woods. I went back to the area and with no light I just swept my hands on the forest floor where I had heard a peculiar sound. I almost couldn't believe that my hand went straight onto an object that as soon as I touched I knew it was my phone. I picked it up thanking the Army for my night training and thanking my brain for being able to make patterns so well from easily forgettable events.

My phone wasn't having much luck around these 24 hours as the next day we had to go into a practice battle lasting a few hours, clearing an old warehouse of enemy that was a good six mile trek away. To get there we had to cross moorland, walls, paths and rivers. Electrical equipment and rivers don't mix so well! Most of the running water around the area was streams, which wasn't a problem as we could walk through and it was only ankle deep. This was a real river and we were going to have to swim. Even in a plastic wallet it was still goodbye time for my phone if it was submerged in this river. I approached the river and thought, well my phone is in my top left jacket pocket, there is nowhere else to put it and I can't refuse to go through the river as I'm not supposed to have my phone on me. I will have to hope it's not so deep and I can walk in it. The call came to go and to start with it was only waist high, then it got deeper and deeper. The freezing water crept up my body and I tried to get on my tip toes to save the phone. The water went up to my chest and literally touched the bottom of my phone in my top left jacket pocket, but it survived. It was a great phone and achieved more than anyone thought possible. What other phones do you know that have survived Army training and filmed the majority of a prime time programme for BBC One?

As well as my equipment I had to have an organised mind to manage my double identity and my own feelings. I had already been called a 'Government experiment' early on in training by one of the Corporals and I had laughed it off. There was a second time this corporal openly talked about me not being not who I said I was that came out of the blue, after I had been there a while and hadn't been questioned for a long time. This wasn't in the BBC programme but was the closest call for me personally. The reason it was so close is that I had almost forgotten about being undercover myself and having been there a while I wasn't in the mode of being prepared to answer questions about who I was. I learned that you can never assume you are safe and ease up just because things are quiet. It happened during a session in the shooting simulator. We had to sit around and wait for others to finish their turn as there were limited spaces to shoot. The corporal was sat next to me for a while and out of nowhere, in front of everyone, he suddenly said 'So, how's your journal going?' After he uttered those words I entered bullet time mode and for the first half a second I genuinely didn't know what he meant and thought he may be referring to a 'best book' that we kept all our training notes in. That probably helped my initial reaction. I realised he was testing me again, commenting I might be a journalist. I hadn't thought about this for ages - Panic! During the next second I decided to go with a reaction based on my genuine confusion and opted to think he meant my best book (even though I knew he didn't). I openly said, 'what, you mean my best book?' He replied, 'No, your journal for who you're working for, who is it, the Sun?' I felt more panicked than I had in previous situations, but managed to shake my head while producing a little laughing sound. He said, 'well ok, the Daily Mail then'. I laughed again but felt an involuntary lump in my throat that I had to swallow. This was the closest anyone came to directly accusing me of being an investigative journalist. I controlled my reactions the best I could by thinking that I genuinely wasn't working for the Sun newspaper or the Daily Mail, so he was actually wrong. I wanted to fight back a bit in the mental stakes as I felt on the back foot. I decided I needed to put an offensive foot forward and be bold. I looked at him and openly went for it by saying, 'That would be pretty cool though' – as if it was an entirely new concept that had entered my head for the first time and being an undercover spy would be a cool thing to do. The mental counter attack must have worked and no-one ever questioned me again after that, even though that corporal had been sharp with his observations of Sharp!

As I had different identities during my time undercover, I couldn't afford for them to cross over or interfere with each other as it might give me away. This was exceptionally difficult, especially as I was constantly between different environments, contexts, and mind states. Once, when I could leave the training environment for the Christmas holiday, I went through the following contexts within the space of 20 hours:

1) Waking up in the middle of a field, training to fight and survive like a soldier.

2) Returning to an Army camp, cleaning kit in a secure military environment where I was half thinking soldier drills and half keeping an ear out for information about bullying.

3) Leaving camp to enjoy freedom and a pint with fellow squaddies in a northern town where I was with all the lads.

4) A train journey down south by myself with time to reflect.

5) The bright lights of Oxford Circus in London bustling with people Christmas shopping.

6) A small quiet BBC office to record my experiences on film and be a professional reporter.

7) A swanky restaurant with BBC executives and then a champagne bar in central London for a night cap.

I didn't really know who I was that day. I was making journalistic notes and secretly filming with the Army lads in the barracks, then only hours later I was inadvertently walking upright and scanning the horizon for danger in busy Christmas time London streets with BBC colleagues. I was always aware of the irony of my behaviour even though at the time I couldn't do much about it. That evening I remember being smartly dressed, but feeling very grubby from waking up in a field in North Yorkshire at 2am. I was walking the streets of Soho amongst the noise, blur and bustle of young fashionable Londoners feeling amazed and humbled at the bright lights of civilization and the happy party goers, but an urge to protect others from drunken disruption or fights. I remember seeing an older drunk man stumbling toward our group and I instantly had a rigid stance and an aggressively protective demeanour and just stared at him as if to say "don't come and mess with us or you know what will happen". I think it was from the mind state you end up in from bayonet training which I guess is a good tool for war, but it doesn't quite work back in civilisation though. I could empathise with why you hear of some squaddies getting involved in a few fights. It's not that they're particularly 'bad lads', it's just their mind-set from training that can spill out in the wrong context after a drink or too. Thankfully I managed to maintain my self-control and bring myself back to being in civilisation fairly quickly! I had to be careful that having a double / triple identity for too long didn't make me go a little bit loopy!

You need time to organise your belongings and your mind well in the first place to stop it getting dis-organised by our chaotic lives.

ENJOYMENT

We all need some space and enjoyment in our lives to give us a break from the intrusive thoughts that enter our mind, to promote positive feelings, and to allow us to just 'be' in the moment and have fun. During activities and hobbies that we really enjoy we can experience what positive psychologists call 'flow'[13]. This might commonly be called 'in the zone' where you are so fully immersed in a feeling of energised focus, involvement and enjoyment at the process of the activity. You are completely absorbed in what you are doing. 'Mindfulness' is subtly different, but similarly involves full focus on the present moment and research suggests a role in psychological well-being[14]. It is the intentional, accepting and non-judgemental focus of one's attention on the emotions, thoughts and sensations occurring in the present moment. It is becoming a commonly heard phrase and practice of it can link to meditation, although it is much wider than

13 *Mihaly Csikszentmihalyi (1990). Flow: The Psychology of Optimal Experience. Harper & Row*

14 *Brown, Kirk Warren; Ryan, Richard M, (2003). The benefits of being present: Mindfulness and its role in psychological well-being. Journal of Personality and Social Psychology, Vol 84(4), 822-848.*

this in its Buddhist traditions. A combination of flow and mindfulness is a great recipe for wellbeing we all need and can be realised in a practical way through a good hobby, a sense of play, openness to our feelings and some personal space and time.

On patrol, soldiers need to space out so they can't be identified as one big blurred lump. My identity was becoming a blurred lump and I felt I needed to get some space from doing both the jobs of an undercover reporter and a training soldier at the same time after a few months. I felt in a relatively good state of mind for the majority of training. However, there was one moment that I knew I needed to take a break as 'reality' was starting to get a little strange. It was a moment where it felt like my sanity started to leak. I was the first to wake up one morning about 5:50am and decided I would drag myself out of bed and use the bathroom first before everyone else got up ten minutes later. I rolled myself out of bed, stood up bleary eyed and pulled a t-shirt on. I grabbed my wash-bag and staggered out the sleeping room into the bathroom. I stood over the sink and turned the tap on. With my eyes still half shut I cupped some water in my hands and splashed my face before rising back up and facing the mirror. As I opened my eyes I suddenly pulled my head back in surprise, opened my eyes wide and stared straight forward. I thought I saw my deceased father staring right back at me. I shook my head and blinked. As I refocused, I saw I was just staring at my own bewildered reflection in the mirror. I relaxed a bit realising my mistake, but stared at the water running down the plug hole in the sink and wondered what my dad would have made of everything if he was still alive. The brain is a strange and wonderful thing. My subconscious was thinking of my father (as it does from time to time being such a significant figure in my life) and as our brains are designed to make meaning and patterns from the abstract, as I looked at a blur with half open eyes in the mirror, my mind had translated my father's face onto my genetically similar features. I wrote about this in my diary as soon as it happened as I wanted to remember the moment. I went to breakfast and carried on with the day but made a note to take it easy and get some space.

I've mentioned chocolate muffins being relaxing and enjoyable for me, but they also were for others. As soon as they had been put out in the dining hall, people were coming back to their tables with about five muffins stuffed in different pockets! We created a saying in our platoon about the 'curse of the two pudding thief'. You were only supposed to take one dessert in the dinner hall and if you got caught with two you'd get a good telling off! It became a great game to try and get two portions and not get found out. Some people went for the tactic of hiding one under the table while you ate the other; some went for the 'I'm getting another for a friend' routine. I preferred the 'tip one bowl into the other and carry out one bowl with two desserts in plan! I did like the strawberry cheesecake and one portion was never enough! In general, I found the food in the Army was good considering how many they had to cater for. You could get as much 'extras' as you wanted and could eat as healthily or unhealthily as you liked. Most of the food tasted pretty good and dinner times were a bit of a source of relaxation as there was nothing to do but eat!

There was a big entertainment centre on camp that a lot of money had been pumped into. It included a snooker and pool table, table tennis table, arcade machines, PCs and games consoles for everyone to use. We spent a bit of time here, but once people had their own game consoles in their rooms we didn't use it that much. Most people would play Call Of Duty on the X-box in the evenings. It was amusing that after training in the Army all day recruits still wanted to play an Army related computer game. I guess we were still itching for action, but without the physical demands. I think training helped our strategic game-play too! Most played games in the evenings despite the fact our Sergeant used to say "Right, go off and do whatever you do in your own time, play naked willy conkers or whatever it is"! No one quite knew what that was, but just the name of it makes you laugh and wince at the same time.

On camp you could buy burgers and fast food in the evening and have a few alcoholic drinks on a Friday and Saturday. No one really got drunk at the bar on camp-usually because no-one had much money. It was just good time to chill out with some fast food, a drink or two, some jokes and either football or boxing on the TV. There was also a few arcade games there and most people either played the quiz machines or one called 'Deer Hunter' that had an infrared plastic shotgun to use. These sorts of occasions brought back a sense of normality. I had to use this normality as a source of continuing my investigation as things heated up. Proper nights out in training were rare as we would either have to work the weekend or people would not have much money and go home. There were a few group nights out in Darlington that I didn't attend as I either took the opportunity to have a proper break and go home, or it wasn't deemed worth it by the production team as there was nothing that I could talk to them about relating to bullying that I couldn't do on camp.

It was great to get my own time off when that came on some weekends. Having to be back for 6pm on a Sunday and only leaving at 5pm on a Friday (or 10pm after I had met my producer and spoken about recent events) only really left me with a day and a half on alternative weekends for 6 months that I could meet up with friends. I would meet up with old friends for a coffee in the day or a beer or two in the evening, maybe play some basketball, see some family, maybe do the odd day trip. I was able to tell friends about the training I had been doing, which was good, but not about all the undercover reporting, which was difficult. I was content however, to just to hear of their stories and be part of normality again for a brief period.

Halfway through training we got to go on an Adventure week! I was with my own platoon all this week and hardly with the corporals (it was a break for them too). There wasn't much going on in terms of the investigation apart from a few racist jokes that were recorded and underlying tensions among peers in our platoon. So, mostly I got to enjoy mountain biking, abseiling, orienteering, caving and climbing around the Yorkshire dales / lake-district area. I had a great sense of achievement from doing abseiling in a quarry. I got a fantastic sense of speed doing mountain biking (downhill anyway!). I scared my senses in narrow caves but combined this with euphoric senses coming out the other side of the cave as we all bonded over the challenge, singing 'Wonder-wall' by Oasis at the top of our voices and hearing it reverberate around cave walls. There were some creative games invented in the cabin too such as sock bowling and long distance sliding down the floor on the mattress competitions! In terms of Army training it was a useful trip for group unity. We got to experience some outdoor pursuits we may never have otherwise and we all achieved a sense of instantly overcoming hard physical challenges whilst admiring the outdoor environment.

Another positive trip within the Army was to France. We went on a long 16 hour coach trip from Catterick to Caen in North France to see real battlefields of history and large military cemeteries. Although we only spent a day in France, we got some military education. It was quite moving standing on a battlefield- knowing that we were in the footsteps of history, bloodshed and the emotion of a battle. In the cemetery, surrounded by all those gravestones of people who had died at war gave me one of those moments of feeling very human, lucky to be alive and appreciative of our existence. The French cemetery provided a philosophical moment for most of the recruits, interrupted of course with dark humour, jokes and inappropriate banter. What is it about a moment of silence that evokes the temptation in some to go against social politeness and social respect and make a squeaky fart noise?!

Although there were good times in the Army, I always had to keep an ear out just in case. That was my job. The more I heard and the quicker I could get it on camera, the quicker I could stop being undercover. Like everyone, time out helped me have energy to refocus.

BEING AWARE / LISTENING

We can all benefit from keeping aware and listening to what is going on around us locally, nationally and globally. The more we are aware of our surroundings and of what is happening within them, the more information we have to make good decisions about our own actions in life. Actively listening (fully concentrating, seeking to understand, responding and remembering information) to others helps relationships and helps us make sense of what is being said.

Sounds alert our attention. If I kept my ear to the ground, it would get dirty. What I meant to say instead of that ridiculous gag, is that in trying to overhear stories and talking to as many people as possible, I hoped I would hear something related to bullying that might give me some direction to continue the investigation.

In my own platoon it was easy to listen out as we were together almost all the time. Good listening and following up on the information is what led me to find out that one of our corporals had urinated on a recruit. We were sat in the shooting simulator and we were taking it in turns to shoot from the prone position (lying down on your front). A recruit who was constantly getting told off for wearing non-military issue shorts under his trousers was lying down and his trousers had come down a little. This revealed bright orange shorts under them. One corporal pointed it out to everyone and started silently laughing. He then took hold of the shorts and yanked them as hard as he could up into the recruit giving him one almighty wedgie, before reminding him not to wear them again. It was all taken as a bit of a joke, but I then heard the recruit next to me say "So now we've seen that corporal throw a bag at someone, give them a wedgie and piss on someone". I had seen the first incidents, but I hadn't seen him 'piss' on anyone. I needed to go and speak to the recruit to whom it happened and to anyone else that had seen it to back up events. I always had to do this as a rule of investigative journalism- try and speak to the victim and get two people to corroborate the story. As it was in my platoon I was able to speak easily to the recruit and actually made use of one of my purpose built secret cameras and not my phone. I had to be careful when talking to recruits like this not to lead with my questioning and try and get as much description as possible. He told me he had indeed been urinated on when he was lying down in the shooting position. He said the corporal had done it on his boot and walked off laughing. This description was shown in the BBC programme.

On another occasion, I overheard a corporal had hit someone in the face during an exercise in the field and had to get testimony. The recruit said he was hit in his respirator (gas mask) and the force went through and hurt the recruit's nose. We had just walked about a mile in our respirators with our heavy bags on while pretending we were escaping a gas attack. We reached a 'decontamination zone' and had to wait in sections in a ditch to be called to be decontaminated. Personally, I couldn't wait to be called as it was hard to breathe with the respirators on and when you've just walked a mile with 70lbs on your back over some moors, all you want to do is breath. When I got to the decontamination line I saw some of my fellow recruits, including one whose nose was bleeding quite badly. I hadn't seen what had happened but instantly heard murmurings that one of our corporals had done it. I couldn't hear reasons why properly at this point but kept trying to listen even though I was being ushered along a decontamination line. I had to wait until the following day until I could really speak to the recruit to find out exactly what happened and why he had been hit and get others in the room to corroborate the story.

I had heard from other recruits in my platoon who had fallen behind in their shooting drills and had a training session with R that they had been hit themselves around the head and that some of the R recruits had said they get hit on a regular basis. I needed to keep my ear out for this and try and get to speak to R recruits wherever possible. I knew some of the faces but not many of their names. I needed to be out of my block and around camp in case I would bump into any of them or over hear conversation. I had regular routines in the evenings where I would walk around and hope for an opportunity. I would walk from my block, past the R block, to the big entertainment centre, to the shop and burger counter and back again via the laundry. I would go past all these places but I would vary the path I took so I was never seen to always be walking the same route. As I was walking, my head would be straight forward but my eyes would be scanning every path, doorway and window for recruit's faces I recognised. My ears would be listening for anything that could relate to the investigation. I tried to always have an excuse for a wander such as going to the laundry, to the shop or for some food. I inadvertently ate a lot of cheese toasties in a popular snack food area just to keep watching out for people. If I hadn't been in the Army when I was having all these cheese toasties, I would have been fat! I'm not sure how many undercover operatives have managed to use cheese toasties as a strategic tool, but it worked for me! Some reports led to nothing, some led to something, some were hanging in the air with potential, but it was hard to get to the right people to hear their story. It did seem that something serious was going on in the R block and I needed to do something to get some more information before I could leave.

Listening is one of the most important skills we need to master and it contributes in a fundamental way to our wellbeing and to the quality of our relations. It can support communication and prevent conflict by understanding one another. It can make other's feel 'heard' which enables comfort, expression and esteem. It helps us have all the information available to problem solve efficiently and with clarity.

Listening is a hard skill as our previous experiences, beliefs, values, assumptions, judgments and bias influence the quality of our listening. Whenever we listen to something, we evaluate what we are hearing and this in turn triggers our emotional reactions and our judgment. If we hear something that contradicts our values or our interests, we tend to react, by becoming defensive; our ability to be effective listeners is hostage of our own filters. It is therefore also important that we are able to listen to ourselves, free from assumptions and judgements. By being self-aware and learning how to listen deeply we can become a catalyst for change.

4:

SUPPRESSING THE ENEMY

"In time of war, when truth is so precious,
it must be attended by a bodyguard of lies"

- *Winston Churchill, Prime Minister.*

PERSISTENCE

Persistence and determination comes from a deep motivation that enables our resilience. It can be really hard to persevere on something when we are tired and feel like we aren't going to be able to achieve what we want and we don't value the goal. If we understand what makes us determined, we can take steps to foster this in ourselves.

Self-Determination Theory[15] (SDT) is a framework conceptualising the motivation which underlies the choices people make.

There are two basic types of motivation: intrinsic and extrinsic. Intrinsic motivation comes from within when the task at hand is inherently interesting, enjoyable, fulfilling, and absorbing. Extrinsic motivation is where you perform activities to reap positive external rewards or to avoid punishment.

Intrinsic motivation facilitates greater concentration, effort, and task completion. According to SDT, this can be developed through feeling competent at an activity, seeing how it connects and relates to other people or goals in life we value and a sense that we can directly influence what is happening with our own actions.

I needed to be perseverant to finish the project. I had hit the DAOR window. This stood for 'Discharge As Of Right' and was the point where you were legally allowed to discharge yourself from employment if you didn't want to be in the Army. The intention was to get in and out before this so we wouldn't have to deal with the complications. I

15 *Ryan, R. M. & Deci, E. L. (Eds.), (2002). Self-determination theory and the facilitation of intrinsic motivation, social development, and well-being. American Psychologist, 55, 68-78. http://dx.doi.org/10.1037/0003-066X.55.1.68*

believe if there had been no evidence, I would have come out at this occasion and the investigation would have disappeared. If I had got categorical or visible enough evidence recorded in this time, we would have decided whether I should leave the Army at this point also. I didn't feel I had yet captured exactly how far bullying went in R, my neighbouring platoon. We had some clear evidence, but were not sure about the extent of the behaviours. We decided to risk it and continue. Whether that was brave or foolish, I passed the official window to leave and for all intents and purposes I was owned by the Army - for four years!

I had to pick the pace up so I went about things in a more systematic and deliberate way. As previously mentioned, my phone came into use on the rifle ranges where no other secret camera I had was able to realistically go. There was one recruit in R who seemed to regularly get hassled. I needed to speak to him but rarely saw him, so I had to take my opportunity while in a shelter on a rifle range one day. It was a space where we rested before shooting and no corporals were around as they were training, scoring or ensuring safety on the firing line. I sat around for a while and engaged in general conversation. There was a few group jokes and nipple tweaking play fights going on! I saw the recruit I had seen have a helmet thrown down onto him and roughly handled go outside for a cigarette. I took my opportunity.

Wandering outside the metal shelter there was a small grassy area. The firing range was mostly blocked from view by a mound of earth and a small country road was the other side slightly obscured by large wooden barriers. It wasn't so unusual to have our phones on us at this stage so I openly got it out and pretended to see if I could get a signal to send a text (some others were doing this). I continued to hold the phone down by my side where it had naturally ended up after sending a text. I pressed record. The recruit spoke to me for a good ten minutes and was open with everything that had been going on. This recruit told me he was hit on an almost daily basis. He said that he and another recruit (who I had spoken to the first time I got my phone out on a firing range) received the worst in the platoon. He said they got beaten up and I asked in a genuinely inquisitive but common tone what he meant by 'beaten up' and he said they were punched and kicked, including in the face. Beyond the physical nature of what he was telling me, a more chilling problem with what was happening came to light. He told me that during training, sometimes he was so scared of what may happen to him if he got something wrong that he couldn't concentrate properly on learning what he was supposed to. I thought this could potentially be disastrous if there is a gap in his knowledge of weapon use. Despite my feelings on some grey areas surrounding bullying, this clearly wasn't right and seemed counter-productive to training. I also got to have a twenty minute conversation with the same recruit a few weeks later in the entertainment complex on camp. I found him on the computers there and it was easy to strike a conversation with him. This time he told me he was beaten in the platoon's bathroom and when he had held his hand up to defend himself from the blows, his finger had been broken. I couldn't tell if it was broken or not when he showed me, but it looked badly injured. He also told me he had been stamped on in a river during bayonet training. He seemed to have psychologically found a way to cope by imagining that it can't be as bad as what the Taliban could do to him. I remember thinking that although Army training needs to be tough, this was clearly the wrong side of the line.

You may well ask "how did people not see you filming them with your phone". In case you're interested in how to secretly film with your phone, remember my 'safety in being bold' saying, it applies here as well. The phone felt like an extension of me, just part of my hand. It was a Nokia N95 and I could get the phone to any state (video record, still camera, voice recorder) and back to the main screen in a second without looking and with it in my pocket. Something that is perhaps not as easy with modern smart phones. Through practice I became adept at holding it stably and naturally, while knowing what angle the lens was pointing at without looking. If I was sitting I would use my lap to rest my arms on, letting my hand relax even though it was holding the phone. If standing, my arms were dropped naturally by my side to look normal and make the camera as still as possible. Additional psychological subtleties of successful secret filming with a phone I used are referenced with my consent in a book about using hidden cameras[16] and listed below as well:

1. Don't look at the phone.

Do not look at the phone – ever – or move it away if someone else looks at it (as tempting as this is). This will only draw attention to it. Practice helps you know where it

16 *Hidden Cameras: Everything You Need to Know About Covert Recording, Undercover Cameras and Secret Filming. Joe Plomin: Jessica Kingsley Publishers; 2016.*

is pointing. It's natural to have a phone in your hand these days so try not to be self-conscious.

2. Consider the lasting memory of your interaction.

Don't go straight in filming; spend some time in normal conversation first. Once you are done, or you feel you have had your phone out too long, put it quietly away back in your pocket and gesture (a lot) with open hands to leave a subtle lasting memory with others that you weren't sat there the whole time with your phone.

3. Use the phone to film openly, when possible.

Spend time openly joking around filming something with your phone – hold the phone camera obviously in a different position to normal and openly and awkwardly. This leaves the impression of what you 'look like' when you are filming (i.e. when you don't look like this – you can't be filming!)

4. Be aware of what or who is behind you when recording.

People behind may be able to see the record screen. Make sure you have your back away from people, or if surrounded use your hand or body naturally to shield straying eyes.

I still needed more from the R platoon. I had got a lot from the one recruit from Ghana, but I needed more perspectives. We weren't really allowed in other platoon's blocks but I wanted a way to get into the R block. I had been asked by the production team at the BBC to try and get some video of the faces of the R corporals to include in the BBC programme. As this was nigh on impossible out in the field I thought it might be easier to get them from their block. I started looking for a way into the lion's den to get video of the corporal's faces or even a chance to talk to any recruits. I stayed on camp one weekend to try and do this. I jumped on a bit of reality that linked my platoon to R platoon and saw a way to twist it to create a seemingly valid reason for me to just walk into their building. Following a trip for training, a couple of the lads in my platoon had lost their bags. They had turned up with R platoon. Unrelated to this, one of those same lads from my platoon had now lost his passport. I thought to myself, what if it had been in his bag and fell out when it got mixed up over at the R block. It was unlikely, but a convenient excuse for one of us to visit their block. If anyone checks up, we really have lost a passport and there is a vague link. It was vague, but it was good enough and time was running out. I spent an hour tooling up. My rituals meant I always had a charged battery and clean spare memory card. I had my trusty phone, another secret camera and hours of filming time. I set off with my story and equipment in hand. I needed to set the cameras to record before I entered the building as it just made it easier and I didn't have to think about making any odd movements in there to turn it on. I went to the shop toilet that was near the R platoon's building, took a breath and pressed record. I stood up straight, rechecked everything was secure in position then marched out of the cubicle, round the corner and up to the block ready to face whatever came my way. I picked up speed and was almost there when I saw an unknown corporal walk in through their door. I stopped, panicked and bottled it. I carried on past the block, back to the toilet cubicle and drew breath whilst feeling annoyed. Back in the shop toilet I wasn't going to let this beat me. Take two; press record, GO. This time I just walked straight up to the door of the block. Once inside I was greeted with a few quiet corridors. It was like a maze of grey with no obvious signs for which way I should go. I kept going up some stairs until I found a door that said R. I hadn't seen anyone until this point and even risked quickly double checking my secret camera was definitely in record mode. I pushed open the R door and went looking for that passport! I walked down another long corridor (sneaking a look at wall displays, door labels and inside open doors as I went) until I first saw a recruit. I just said the first thing that came into my head- 'Alright mate, are your Corporals in?' When he replied no, I gave a look of disappointment as I wanted to ask them about the missing passport, but in my head I was secretly relieved I didn't have to deal with them. I asked the recruit (who I kind of recognised but had never spoken to before) about a missing passport and he said he would go and check. He left me alone in the corridor while he did this. It gave me 30 seconds to scope the rest of the place out. I worked out where the bathroom was, where the different sections had dorm rooms and where the corporal's and sergeant's office was. Their door was closed so I couldn't sneak a peek. The walls of the corridors were plain and showed no photos so I couldn't get any information or pictures. I suddenly had a chance to speak to R recruits in comfortable surrounds for a bit longer than just passing. I walked into the room where the recruit was asking around and I recognised a couple of people, one of whom I had met when I pledged my allegiance to the Queen. I started making chit chat and talking about how training was going.

I managed to get some information from this recruit. The majority was going over things I already knew, but seeing if he had a more detailed picture of what happened. He seemed open and happy to talk to me. I didn't get a great deal of new information, but I found out that their platoon had an investigation for bullying by other professionals in the Army following a complaint from one of the recruits. The recruit I spoke to wasn't sure of the outcome of the investigation but knew one of the corporals was no longer training with them. Worryingly, he also told me that one of the Corporals had been allowed to stand around the lads while they were filling in questionnaires relating to how their corporals treated them. I started to feel I had been there too long and the recruit I was talking to was getting picked up to go out of camp as it was the weekend. I left wondering how I was going to continue to fully understand what was going on in the R platoon without me being part of them.

I studied our future timetable well and it was usually put up three to four weeks in advance. I kept seeing potential opportunities to experience the R corporals or possibly be put next to R platoon so I could try and speak to them further. We went for a week of machine gun training at a place called Altcar in Liverpool. Typically, we were accommodated in different blocks and during the day we would all sit separately on the open fields as we all practiced with light machine guns. When I wasn't shooting or having to move the target boards up and down for those who were shooting, I would sit with my platoon on the frosty grass with the sound of 20 sets of machine guns loudly going rat-a-tat-tat whilst looking over at R platoon thinking how I could speak to them. I could see them, but I knew if I waltzed over and started chatting I would get told in no uncertain terms by one of their corporals to get back over to my side. It was very frustrating. I managed a few more snatched conversations to build evidence, but no real substance on camera and no footage of bullying happening.

The same happened on the trip to France and even though we were in the same areas we were still separate. On the one occasion we had an hour to properly mix I saw a good opportunity when two lads from R platoon separated to go up a monument and overlook the sea. I managed to wander over, break the ice and rapidly bring up conversation about their corporals without leading any conversation. I hoped this would be a good conversation and the trip won't be wasted. Unfortunately there was another variable I couldn't control being on the coast – The wind! I was able to think about using my body to shield the wind at first, but when the recruit came to talk about his corporals and what he had experienced in relation to bullying he moved to a position where I had to leave the phone exposed to the elements. I hoped I would be ok, but when listening back all I got was a loud fuzzy sound. I had made a note of what he said so it was more evidence, but it couldn't be used in the programme even though we considered getting a lip reader to subtitle it for us!

I was sick of waiting for lucky meetings so I even tried to pro-actively create a big group event for us all. We did like to enjoy the occasional game of football on weekends if we had time and the corporals had previously arranged a match against another platoon. It occurred to me, why not play R platoon! A bit more of an informal setting could build up our relationships and be a good chance to speak to them and see their corporals. It seemed like a brilliant move and I was hopeful. I asked my corporal one day if he could organise a match against R platoon for us and got a short reply just saying 'maybe'. Less than a week later, we got told we were playing R platoon in a football match! I was taken a-back as the plan seemed to work so easily (too easily). It was also great to see recruits requests were listened to and acted upon quickly. I felt like a scumbag because the corporals were kindly doing things for me (us) but it was done without their full knowledge of why I asked.

I was ready to go, but unfortunately rivalry got in the way. The Army is naturally a competitive place and this competition between platoons is a driving force in your own progression. When we got to the football pitch, R platoon had come alone. This was bad in one way as I couldn't see their corporals, but good as it meant I could hopefully ask questions freely. The problem was, they stood in a dug-out on one side of the field and we stood in a dug-out on the other side. Yet again, I could see them but not speak to them. I tried to speak to a couple of them on the pitch when the ball had gone over the fence and was being retrieved, but there was no way I could carry a phone or any other secret camera I had onto the pitch in these moments and look normal. It was pretty much useless apart from getting my face more familiar to them and visa-versa. This was typically the way it went with getting evidence from R platoon.

I had one last lead to follow up on and a chance to get more detail to one of the first incidents I heard about. I found out that a recruit who left the R platoon and was waiting to be transferred was still being given work on camp, but in a different building. I only had a description of him and where he usually worked in the day so I made a point of wandering past this area and hoped I could see him. After a few false alarms, a recruit who fitted the description walked right past me in the spot I had been told he worked. I was surprised, but sure it was him. I couldn't speak to him then, so just made sure I noted his face, body shape and walk so I could pick him out later on. A few days later when I was hunting for recruits to speak to in the evening I recognised him in the entertainment complex. I established that he had a regular routine of hanging out there and using the cinema room. Suddenly, I became much more interested in the films they were showing! It took me a few attempts of sitting in the room near him until it felt natural to speak. I didn't want to scare him off or just get another snatched conversation as this was one of my last shots. On the first reasonable chance we had to talk properly, conversation cropped up about the film that was on. There were not many other people in the room this night either which helped. We got talking and I managed to use the tops of chairs to naturally rest my hand and my phone so I could film our conversation. I captured some useful information about him being hit by a Corporal near the start of training. This moment just about made it into the BBC programme, but we had to explain why it was so dark and why loud sound effects were in the background! I tried to catch him outside of the room but the set up never warranted me filming and talking about evidence.

I had been as persistent as I could and got the majority of footage and evidence I could from inside the training facility. The psychologist in me still really wanted to get to the bottom of understanding why certain behaviour related to bullying had occurred so it might be prevented in the future.

THE IMPACT OF CULTURE

The culture we are part of at a global, national or local level affects how we think and how we act. To be resilient we need to be aware as possible of how these cultures affect us and be able to critically reflect on what may be helpful and what may constrain us.

A meme is an idea, behaviour, or style that spreads from person to person within a culture[17]. A meme acts as a unit for carrying cultural ideas, symbols, or practices that can be transmitted from one mind to another through writing, speech, gestures, rituals, or other imitable phenomena with a mimicked theme. Memes provide an opportunity to connect with people of all sorts and encourage participation and sharing. They have the ability to be shared across a wide range of platforms and in the modern day on the internet and smart phones. Memes encourage collaborative community while also cultivating a new form of discourse. They can start small and quickly go 'viral' where they take on a life of their own and no-one has control over them.

I felt memes were important to understanding how cultures in the Army were passed on. I wanted to try and understand some of the behaviours of the corporals and what life was like for them as much as I could, so I could understand the impact on training recruits in greater depth. The corporals assumed many roles that

17 *Dawkins, Richard (1989), The Selfish Gene (2 ed.), Oxford University Press, p. 192, ISBN 0-19-286092-5*

included being shouting and menacing, instructional, jokey, nurturing and caring and reflective. I had seen our corporals in different contexts within the Army and seen many different sides to them that weren't all able to be presented within the time limitations of the BBC programme.

Some lessons we learned just through listening to the experiences of our corporals and the emotion they told the stories with. I remember one of our corporals telling us a story about how to handle the light machine gun (LMG). It was in the context of telling us how to clear a jam if the firing mechanism for the LMG gets stuck. Essentially, you have to get a friend to wrap a belt around the cocking handle and as you point the weapon forward he tugs as hard as possible from behind. He told us the worst mistake to make when trying to un-jam the weapon, that his friend had learned the hard way. The mistake his friend made was to turn the weapon upwards and stamp down on the cocking handle- releasing several rounds into his head. I can't do it justice in written words, but the emotion on the corporal's face was a lesson to us all and I don't think anyone messed around with this weapon after.

I agree that training has to be tough to prepare for the hard work, however, I think there is a culture among some that take things too far when it isn't needed for recruits to learn. Personally, I felt I was trained well by the Army and I hope I was seen as a good recruit at the time. I wasn't kicked or punched to learn my lessons. Some corporals would argue I didn't need to be, because I was already fairly mature and able when I started. These same corporals or other members of training staff voiced an opinion several times informally that on some occasions they felt a 'filling in' was the best way to help some recruits learn. They would mean roughing up a recruit with a 'bad' or 'lazy' attitude and I felt they said this in a way that they thought they would be genuinely helping the recruit. Instead of getting caught up in the debate of the 'rightness' or 'wrongness' of this, I am interested in why this view exists (also believed by members of the public) that on some occasions a recruit may need to be slapped around a bit to improve their attitude or ability. This is a behaviouristic view of learning and focussed on developing external motivation, rather than a deeper form of critical thinking and internal motivation. There is an argument that in the context of the Army you need people who respond like robots to orders, even though this is de-humanising outside of this context. The counter to this is that soldiers need to be able to think for themselves if they are without any senior staff. It is inescapable that a high proportion of recruits and corporals at Catterick training centre were from economically deprived areas with minimal education. I wondered about increased exposure to violence around these environments and its transfer into the view that violence is normal and can help some recruits learn in the Army. I wondered if aggressive cultures were replicated and magnified within the Army context from experiences training staff have had in their personal backgrounds as well as their professional backgrounds. It is likely that if they had been treated aggressively while they were training that this meant they felt it was appropriate to do to others. There was a normalisation of aggression and violence that is perhaps expected in the context of war and the Army as a whole, but was unexpected for fellow humans training together in a workplace.

During my training in the Army, it felt like there was an acknowledgement of the rules and theory of the Army's policy on bullying, but there was also an accepted culture on the ground and in practice that didn't quite gel with what society and the Army as an organisational system may deem 'good practice'. I realised that some things sound 'wrong' if you have never been in the Army, but can feel 'right' when you are in that environment. I could therefore see why some incidents of violence in training go unreported. I will use my own experience to explain this so as not to unjustly involve anyone else. There was one occasion when we were learning how to attack enemy positions at night. This was the first time we had done this and the dark moorland was full of scurried activity as trainee soldiers ran into positions at the top of a wooded hill. When gunfire kicked off, the adrenaline kicked in and my section took up a firing position on top of a grassy slope. It seemed there were multiple enemies and as it was dark it was hard to tell what was going on! A few of us saw the unmistakable flashes of gunfire amongst the trees, so we shot in that direction. As soon as we had, we heard screaming and cursing from our platoon commander who was watching. In all the confusion, we had shot at our own men! In the moment, I was horrified at what I had done and thankful we were only practicing using blank rounds. The platoon commander came running over to us yelling at us to stop firing. I was lying down on the ground in the firing position and as he approached me at speed, I looked up and I thought he was going to continue towards me and kick me in the chest. I tensed my stomach to receive a swift boot. However, the platoon commander stopped as he got to us and continued to shout at us for our mistake and point out where the real enemy was. I stopped tensing my stomach and worked hard with the rest of my platoon to clear the enemy position and finish the practice drill. In that moment, I don't think I would have complained if I had been kicked (assuming I was not an undercover reporter and I was in the Army for real). I wouldn't have complained because I felt so awful about what I had done that I felt I would have 'deserved' a kick. At the same time I didn't need to be kicked to learn my lesson here. I would have killed my own comrades and have to live the consequences if it had been real. Reflecting on this made me determined to never make that mistake again. I felt this was a grey area in the culture that may not matter in some instances where there was no malicious intent, but may mask someone with an unpleasant nature who took violence to an extreme. The line between the two can be hard to determine in the heat of the moment. The feeling that I 'deserved it' is something that resonated with what some other recruits told me about themselves being beaten and not complaining.

Worrying to me was that the culture in Army training produced a reaction in me where I felt the urge to hit someone. It was an important moment for me to reflect on to help understand the culture in the Army and why some incidents that may be deemed as bullying occur. On this occasion we were running the steeple chase which was a mile and a half of rough terrain, freezing water pits, jumps and mud glorious mud! On sunny days I quite enjoyed it. On freezing winter days, I did not. In this session, we had to run through it a second time because we were too slow and people were missing out water pits. I was exhausted after doing it twice, but we were made to do it a third time as people were again seen missing out water pits. I was running behind a recruit who even on this third time was missing out jumps and water pits when he thought he wasn't being watched. Putting aside my annoyance that he was beating me because he was missing out the jumps, the real frustration was that if he was seen we would ALL have to go round a fourth time. Corporals knew people try and miss out jumps and are very watchful from a distance. Running the steeple chase three times was very tough and I had no desire to do it another time. We finished the third lap and I was just behind the recruit who had been running around water pits again. We had to wait for others to finish, but as I crossed the line I felt an overwhelming desire to slap him hard around the head and tell him why he shouldn't miss out jumps so we didn't ALL have to go again. This was a new experience for me as I'm usually very calm. It struck home when I thought that in the years of working with some of the most challenging behaviour from young people in Leeds with complex social and emotional needs, I had never once felt any urge to hit any of them to change their behaviour. The urge to hit someone to change their behaviour was against any set of professional and personal values I have ever had, but in that moment, in that environment, I can't deny I felt the need to 'educate' someone by hitting them so they would know how serious I was about what I had to say. The only thing that stopped me giving him a slap round the head was the fact that I knew if I did, it would have effectively been the end of the investigation and I would have no moral ground to stand on. In the end I told the recruit what I thought anyway and I hoped this made him think twice next time. I felt I could understand how actions of violence don't always stem from the innate disposition of that person (i.e. they are a 'bad' person) but from the environment, culture and increased testosterone levels. This can be widened out from this Army experience to other environments and cultures in more everyday life situations and is something we need to be aware of and compassionate to, in order to go towards reducing cyclical cultures where violence can create violence.

There was one moment in relation to violence, culture, words and their impact, where I felt a sickening physiological reaction in me. I felt it had the potential to cause death to many innocent lives. This was not 'bullying' in any physical sense and there was no visible effect of it at the time. It was only words that were said, but it was said by someone in a position of responsibility to impressionable ears.

Nine words with potentially massive implications:

"And that's how you get away with war crimes".

This occurred during a training session outside as we were being taught how to clear buildings of hostile people. The lessons were long and tactical. It's the type of training that gets the adrenaline going as your moving quickly along narrow stone corridors, weapon poised, ready to swing round a corner and unleash a few rounds at enemy hiding in a corner. We used an old stone infrastructure that had no roof or windows but matched the layout of a small house with a few corridors and open rooms. We also learnt how to use smoke grenades to cover our entry to the building and commands and signs for others to let them know our situation within the building. The corporal training us made serious comments making me think about the harsh reality of having to clear these sorts of buildings. The corporal spoke about bullets not discriminating for age and made us brutally aware that in certain circumstances you may have to kill children; especially in certain countries where child soldiers are becoming more common and will kill you. It's a horrible thing to think, but if a 10 year old who has been trained by the enemy is stood pointing a weapon at you, a moment's hesitation because of their age may cost you your life. The Army's dark humour re-emerged and the corporal spoke of enemies popping their heads up on roof tops and if we spotted them we were to 'give them the good news' (i.e. shoot them!). It may not sound funny here, but it made me laugh in the moment along with other recruits. In the midst of this, the corporal told us sometimes you may have to shoot many people in the building and that it is the soldier's perspective of a threat that counts as to whether you shoot or not. He added the comment at the end "...and that's how you get away with war crimes" while smiling and slightly laughing. There are several interpretations possible for his expression of this phrase, it may have been in jest, but when I heard this comment I got a sick feeling in my gut that such a throw away statement given by an authority figure could result in recruits developing an attitude that it is ok to kill innocent people in the context of clearing a building as in reality no-one will know. Although it is practically not possible to link one comment to another person's actions years later, I could envisage in principal that innocent people may get killed in the future because of words like these in the training scenario being internalised and contributing to a soldier's way of being. This was mentioned in the BBC programme.

I can see when clearing buildings, unintentional killing of innocent people may happen as difficult decisions have to be made instantly among confusion. This is different from a disregard for people's lives when they pose no threat. If an attitude is created where soldiers believe it's all too easy to kill and no-one will ever know, and violence and hatred is normalised, then in a certain situation this may manifest in dehumanising of others and innocent people losing their lives. I wanted to make my thoughts clear on this, not to demonise anyone without giving thought to the complex emotions and psychological effects war can have on peoples actions, but to make clear my feelings about this moment so awareness is raised about off-hand comments made by authority figures in the Army (or any organisation) and highlight the care and responsibility that I feel needs to be evident when teaching impressionable people. Culture affects how we all think and behave. Whether this is Army culture, an office culture where you work, street culture where you live or national culture, we need to be critically reflective of how we are affected and take steps not to contribute to cultures that may oppress others. Words affect cultures and powerful media cooperation's can spread words quicker than anyone. We all have a responsibility to each other.

CREATIVITY AND OPTIONS

There are times we all need change for our wellbeing. We have more possibilities for change if we have options. The more creative we can be, the more options we have. Creativity embraces originality and makes unique connections between seemingly disparate ideas. Creativity is about living life as a journey into seeing and communicating the extra-ordinary in the simplest, most every day acts. The greater the capacity to produce ideas that are both original and adaptive, the more we can adjust to novel circumstances and to solve problems that unexpectedly arise. This capacity is often very valuable for our resilience in everyday chaotic life. Some individuals are fortunate that their sprouting imagination was nurtured and grown into strong creative thinking abilities, but the seeds of creativity live in everyone. 'Thinking outside of the box' is something everyone can develop and is a skill.

It was getting perilously close to the time I would finish training and it was decided by the production team that it was time to get me out and that I had got enough evidence to make the BBC programme with. I could continue to get more, but the process of leaving could be long and I would still have time to investigate while this was happening. It would be difficult to use the excuse that the Army just wasn't for me, as I was performing well as a recruit. We had to come up with a very good excuse for why I needed to leave and why I would be no good as a soldier if I stayed. I needed a helping hand. Re-enter my 'girlfriend' Susan. We decided that the weekends off camp together had been eventful and that Susan was pregnant. I was going to be a dad!

Morally and ethically this felt on a knife edge and of all my deception, I felt worst about this one. In my mind there were actually only two areas I was deceptive about during my time in the army. One was my wish to join the Army in the first place and the second was anything to do with my girlfriend Susan. Neither was pleasant. However, we could see no other viable alternative and this felt like it had the best shot of working at the time.

I went about creatively making my real memories again: where we were, what it was like, the bedroom, the moment she lay down on the bed. I envisaged the strange phone call to ask to speak to me a couple of months after, how she told me she was pregnant and where I was. I felt the surprise and mixed emotions of joy and worry and imagined the arguments about me being in the Army and trying to raise a child. In a version of reality in my head, it had happened. I was ready to put the plan into action. Back at camp I went for a burger one evening with one of the recruits I considered a good friend during my time there. The other recruit told me he had some news. He told me he had got his girlfriend pregnant! I was happy for him and felt bad that I had planned to use the story of a situation like this as an excuse to leave the Army and he was living it for real. I rang the production team and we considered changing the plan, but couldn't think of an alternative. The recruit seemed to ultimately be ok with having the child anyway while staying in the Army, so he wasn't going to tell the corporals and deal with it later on in his personal life. This meant I could probably go ahead with it as an excuse. I felt nervous at this point because I knew as soon as I said anything to training staff the following events wouldn't be fully in my control. I would have to go back to living on the edge and reacting quickly to anything thrown at me that may test my undercover story. I hoped they wouldn't smell straight through the excuse and realise that my whole time with them in Army training had all been for an alternative reason. I went upstairs in my block, into the office and told the Sergeant. The conversation was short and to the point, but it got the ball rolling. He asked me to go away and sleep on it and write a letter as to why I wanted to leave for the platoon commander who I could speak to soon. I knew the message would go around the other corporals and recruits quickly. For the next two weeks in training I made myself feel and look slightly dishevelled and tired. I began to get comments about not being my 'usual' self because of what has happened. The usual conflicting thoughts went through my head of feeling pleased people seemed to be buying what I was saying and feeling like a b**tard for making people believe and feel things for me that weren't true. It felt worse when the corporals in my platoon (particularly my section commander) were incredibly nice towards me when they thought I was in this difficult situation. I didn't like the negative emotions I knew they would feel towards me when they found out, but had to willingly accept them as part of the process. I went through a series of about seven interviews at various stages of the process. Some in my platoon, some with a voluntary organisation designed to help soldiers having babies. I tried to always give a sense that I did still want to be in the Army deep down and I wasn't making this decision easily, but also that I felt it was best for me and my 'future family' if I left. I reeled out the same story at every interview and received back the stories of all those in the Army who have children and do well, the help you can get if you have children in the Army and offers of marriage quarters to live in with a crèche for the child. I listened to everyone but remained steady in my position. I made it through all the preliminary interviews to finally get an interview with the commanding officer of the Kings Division who would ultimately decide my fate. However, the first date when I could see him occurred when my platoon would be away on 'Final Exercise'- a five day scenario out in the field that put everything we had learned in training to the test. As it was up in Scotland, no-one could bring me back and I had to go with everyone, complete the exercise and wait until the week after. So off to bonnie Scotland it was!

I spent 4 nights and 5 days at Garelochhead training facility. I tried to give it my all to support team morale and help the others do well in the exercise, despite feeling a little on the social outskirts as everyone knew I was going. I was worried I would be treated differently, but this was just in my own head and I was treated just like everyone else. There were a few friendly comments among the five days from platoon staff saying "how can you give this life up" when things had been exciting. This was their last attempt to get me to stay. I pushed myself hard on this last exercise as some sort of guilt driven personal punishment for my deception. I felt a sense of belonging to the platoon by this time, as did everyone by this stage from everything we had been through as a group, but everyone was about to go their separate ways anyway when training finished. We were mostly left to our own devices in the final exercises as we didn't need much direction anymore. We built our sleeping area and kept watch at all times. The only time the corporals joined us was when we were doing specific patrols or activities such as ambushes. Having done essentially all of Infantry training in the British Army, I sat gripping my rifle in the misty Scottish forest, feeling prepared for any enemy attacks. We patrolled the mountains and forests with stealth and deadly precision. I felt like I was a soldier. But I wasn't. I knew that, and in a way I couldn't wait to stop pretending.

The last morning on the exercise saw a large battle against enemy in a vacant warehouse and we joined with R platoon (who we had been totally separate from for the 5 days) to jointly take control of the location. It was a tiring and fierce battle. We had to pick up all the thousands of empty shell casing after we finished which was annoying, but we were treated to a full fry up breakfast as a reward. After five days on rations, an early morning six mile patrol and explosive gun fight in a warehouse, those sausages and bacon tasted amazing!

I stood staring at a plain wooden office door in the officer's building waiting for my final interview. I never really felt under any real suspicion throughout this leaving period, but almost as soon as I walked into the final interview the commanding officer bluntly said "So, you went home one weekend and cooked up a plan to get your girlfriend pregnant to get out of the Army did you?". This took me aback slightly, but went on the offensive by maintaining eye-contact and looking back in a slightly offended way simply saying, "no sir". During the rest of the conversation I could see he didn't really think this is what I had done and was perhaps just used to checking recruit's plans to get out of the Army. He seemed to buy everything and he even agreed with my plight at the end saying it *was* the right decision for me to leave even though I had performed well as a recruit. That moment was music to my ears. The stamp went on the paper and it was official. I could leave. Well, as soon as I had completed all the endless administration tasks. This would take another 2 weeks, which would mean I would be leaving just one week short of completing the whole six months of basic infantry training.

I spent the last few days in a clearing house with other recruits who were leaving the Army for numerous reasons. The upkeep of the building was poor as it was just temporary accommodation. I kept wandering back up to my old platoon and even sat helping to clean their weapons with them for a couple of hours one day. This was probably another attempt at diminishing my guilt for my deception. I got all the leaving administration tasks done including a final medical to check I hadn't had any adverse health effects from Army training. During this time the Doctor was the only other person who really questioned the situation and gave me a sarcastic comment with a raised eyebrow about my "relatively mature girlfriend" getting pregnant "by *accident* in this modern day and age". My fellow recruits would complete training and call themselves soldiers just days after I would leave. Although I was disappointed not to join in their achievement having gone through it all with them, I'm glad I didn't do the final parade as I would have felt like more of a fraud than I was. I felt proud of them and glad they got to have their day without anything I did spoiling it for them.

The day came when I was scheduled to leave. I kept thinking something had to go wrong because it had all worked a bit too smoothly so far. Even in the last few minutes walking towards the gate for last time, I still thought something else might happen to stop me leaving. I even started getting paranoid thoughts of the film 'The Truman Show' and wondered if the whole thing was set up just to see how someone copes with 6 months undercover in the Army. I got my thoughts of Keyser Söze back when walking through the gate for the last time. Given we were making a TV programme I tried to capture this moment on film and quickly turned my phone camera on myself to show my face with the gate behind as I walked away to freedom with a relieved yet joyful sigh. I recorded a piece to camera in the car as soon as I got in and you can see the relief on my face. I had mixed feelings of leaving as it had become a way of life for me. I had made some genuine attachments and had some positive memories and rewarding experiences as well as tough, arduous, confusing and lonely ones. I drove away taking one last long look at the camp gates through the raindrops on the window of my car.

Making sense of the undercover experience would take some time. Creativity is something that enables our meaning making in the world, as well as supporting relaxation and problem solving. It can help get thoughts and feelings that are difficult to articulate out of our heads. Creativity is a set of skills, an attitude to life and the ability to have original, meaningful ideas that often cross over disciplines and connect previously separate information. Like all skills, creativity needs nourishing and exercising. Creative activities are numerous and are only limited by our imagination. Typically they might be around art and crafts, drawing, poetry, acting and play. My own attempt at writing rhymes as a form of creative expression following the undercover experience is shown in the appendix.

There is a particular kind of upward spiral for wellbeing and creativity[18] engaging in creative behaviour leads to increases in wellbeing the next day, and this increased wellbeing is likely to facilitate creative activity on the same

---

18 1.Tamlin S. Conner, Colin G. DeYoung, Paul J. Silvia. Everyday creative activity as a path to flourishing. The Journal of Positive Psychology, 2016; 1 DOI: 10.1080/17439760.2016.1257049

day. Everyday creativity is a means of cultivating positive psychological functioning. It's a vital ingredient of being human, leading to growth, change and progress at an individual and societal level.

5:
THE ATTACK

"Wars of pen and ink often lead to
wars of cannon and bayonets"

- *Edward Counsel, Maxims.*

MANAGING CHANGE

Change is inevitable. I would go so far as to say that we are never not changing. The interactions between ourselves, our environment and our brains over time is constantly altering in different ways, some imperceptible and some more obvious. We all can find change hard as we are predisposed to seek some level of predictability, stability and control over our lives. Transitioning from one place to another, or experiencing loss of some form can be a challenge that provokes anxiety as we take our previous experiences with us and try and assimilate them with our new experiences in a way that feels meaningful.

The Army wasn't going to be out of me for a while. It couldn't be yet anyway because I still couldn't tell my friends what I was really doing in case it unintentionally got leaked to the Army. To my friends, I had completed training and gone to join my battalion in the Yorkshire regiment. It gave me an excuse for not being available during the week. When I was in the Army I could tell people real things I had been doing. Now, I had to make up where I was during the week and completely fabricate Army activities I had been involved in to tell my friends when they asked how my week was. This meant part of 'Russell' was actually still in the Army!

To get more video of myself and the corporals in training, I had to pretend to want the 'passing out' DVD (final ceremony) for the R platoon as well as my own. I had to call up the person who filmed them and go to his house to pick up the DVD and pay for it. This also included footage of bayonet training. I obtained footage from my platoon from a fellow recruit who I met following leaving the Army. I considered him a friend and saw the job as separate to this, but for him I can see how it would be hard to extricate the two once he knew the full story. When I met this recruit to get the video off him, my double lives clashed together. The recruit knew I had left the Army whereas my older friends thought I was still in the Army. I stood up from the table we were sat at to get a drink and all of a sudden I saw an old school friend looking at me. I did one of those bullet time moments again where my first reaction was to panic, but then seemed to have an in-depth mental planning meeting that was probably only a second in reality. It was a busy pub and quite noisy and I instinctively stepped towards my school friend and put my body in between him and my soldier friend. The soldier friend could see I was talking, but I kept my body as a barrier and didn't introduce them. I had a conversation at a tone low enough so that my soldier friend couldn't hear over the rest of the noise. It was tense, but I managed to keep my narratives separate even though they were grinding up against each other like a runaway high speed train against a wall.

Now all my extra undercover activities were done, my job continued into the editing process of the BBC programme for almost another five months. I was involved with the production team every day from now on and the fact I had managed to get myself discharged from the Army meant we could take our time in developing the BBC programme. After months of physical drills, getting up at dawn and crawling in mud, I took great pleasure in being in an edit suite and drinking well prepared coffee whenever I wanted, sitting on a large leather sofa and having biscuits and fruit brought to the room. The edit suite was fairly large and had a couple of computers in as well as the main editing computer. There was a table in the middle for food and drinks and a nice red carpet. I learned a lot about the editing process from the editor who did a very good job with the material we had in terms of trying to make a story as coherent as possible. I was needed so I could be asked who was who, what the footage was and other factual issues with what was being put together. There was quite a lot of banter and laughter throughout the early stages of this process and it felt good to be able to interact properly with work colleagues again in a non-military environment and to be able to do things like having a quick drink after work or have a long lunch. Not being shouted at for not ironing your shirt properly was pretty cool as well!

Having not been in an edit suite before, I wanted to play with the special effects buttons but was very sensibly discouraged as it was a serious BBC programme. I had my views of what would be appropriate sound tracks and favoured the melodically sombre, powerful, masculine and military like beat of several hip-hop tracks. I had several songs that would play in my head while on long runs in the Army for my own motivation. When I heard sentiments of self-determination in the lyrics from rappers such as Jay-Z, combined with a hard marching beat, it somehow made me grit my teeth a bit more and make me feel like I had a renewed sense of energy flowing through me. I managed to convert the editor I was working with to go to a Lupe Fiasco concert after he included several instrumental versions of his songs in the BBC programme following my suggestion. We used the obviously titled 'Soldier' track by Eminem for the credits of the BBC programme. The haunting repeated vocal of

'I'm a soldier' along with a solid baseline, brisk beat and melancholic electronic organ riff seemed to resonate with my inner voice when I was undercover telling myself I *was* a soldier. We also used Dr Dre's 'The Watcher', because at times that was definitely how I saw myself and my role undercover; silently watching the reality of life there and whispering among background bangs.

There was other work I did in this time of transition from the Army to Media life that I found valuable and interesting. I got to work with a voice coach as I would be voicing over the BBC programme and practicing for TV/Radio interviews that we thought I may have to do upon release. The voice coach helped me think about my posture, how I breathed when I spoke, how to convey the meaning and feeling of the story I was telling and how to bring the audience in. Practice for potential interviews was something that was running alongside everything else in my work diary at this point. I felt a certain amount of pressure that I was carrying the whole project into the public at a point when I felt I didn't quite have the overall picture sewn up in my head or had fully made sense of all my experiences. In order to feel what it would be like being filmed in context, I was able to use contacts of the production team to go and watch the Today Programme on BBC Radio 4 go out live, The Breakfast programme being filmed for BBC 1 and Newsnight being filmed for BBC2 (as well as work for them for a day). I also stood in the One Show studio while it was being filmed and got to open a door for Christine Bleakley (who very politely thanked me and smiled) and was involved in a conversation with Matthew Wright (guest hosting that day) who was talking about his holidays!

Over and above the TV programme, I was more than ready to let the world know what had happened and put everyone on the same page so I could feel like myself again. About sixteen months after I had originally joined the BBC to go undercover in the Army, the time came to let the Ministry of Defence know what was going to happen (or more to the point, what had just happened for the last year!). Having been undercover so long with lack of proper peer support, the thing I was craving the most was telling my friends. It was close to a year and a half I had not been wholly truthful to them. This did go on for too long in hindsight. I had mentally signed off the six months in the Army to keep secrets from my friends, but not the five months after as well. I started to become quite down and felt stuck in limbo even though there was a lot going on to keep me busy. You may recognise the feeling if you have struggled to reconcile change and transition in your life and make sense of your past and present. Having no true sense of belonging is difficult at this time and something we all seek. When we are struggling, having one secure base or consistent factor (such as good friends and family) can help us while we assimilate our thoughts and identity to the new situation we face. There is no one way to manage change and we actually all do this efficiently on a day to day basis in many ways. The more significant changes may take some time and benefit from some elements of security to hold onto, but we manage them. We are all here because our human species is adaptable in a changeable world.

MAINTAINING INDIVIDUALITY IN COMPLICATED SYSTEMS

A system or organisation will ultimately want to prioritise its own existence. If you are part of a large organisation or system in your work, you are a cog in the mechanism. You may be a key cog, but are just one small element of the larger picture that can be replaced. We are all small cogs in the wide eco-system of the planet and the universe. This can be both motivating (we are contributing to something special and belong somewhere) and diminishing (we don't have a positive identity or sense of uniqueness) at the same time. The psychological tension can cause uncomfortable feelings. Recognising systems we are in, while at the same time having a sense of being an important part of them is important for our esteem and resilience.

A BBC executive producer rang the MOD and told them what we had done and that a BBC programme was set to go out. The two large public sector organisations were now openly involved in dialogue around the project and I was an individual in the middle of this. I was significant, yet insignificant at the same time as the senior members of each organisation were more directly involved in managing the situation.

I was nervously sat back in the edit suite wondering what was going to happen to me from this point on. I didn't have too much time to contemplate my fate as things soon went into hyper-drive. The UK's broadcast regulations require the BBC and other broadcasters to offer the subjects of an investigation or report an opportunity to respond to allegations about them. This could take the form of an interview or a statement. In the event – the Army opted for an interview. Lord Dannatt defended the Army's position saying the Army had improved with regards to their fight against bullying. He said it was difficult to get rid of bullying all together in a large organisation and that there were always going to be a few 'bad apples'.

The team openly went around ex-recruit's houses that were in K or R platoon. It was a hectic few days and a lot of information was corroborated but nothing new came to light. I also had my first role as a TV interviewer. I went to speak to Dominic Christopher-Baskeyfield, who had been hit on the head by a Sergeant throwing his drill stick at him, resulting in a blood clot. We filmed this around a fishing pond and as the production team set up the cameras I took the time to get to know Dominic. The key messages that were used in the BBC programme were obtained in the first few minutes of speaking.

At the same time as all this was going on I was also finally able to try and get round family and closest friends to tell them in person what had happened. I was able to use my phone and Facebook to tell other friends who I had not managed to get to see. The BBC also started to put out some trailers on BBC1 of me whispering from the drying room in the Army barracks to promote the BBC programme. I remember getting quite a few texts from people who were more than a bit surprised at me randomly popping up on their screen telling them that I had been undercover in the Army for 6 months investigating bullying and politely inviting them to watch the story!

In some ways, telling people was a bit of an anti-climax. It was a moment I had looked forward to for so long, but as things were so hectic I couldn't take any time with it. I was also in one of those states where I wasn't really feeling much emotion as I was so overwhelmed with everything going on around me and feeling apprehension about what would happen when the BBC programme actually went out.

The story also broke in the Daily Mail Newspaper shortly after the Army were told. The story had been buried away in the paper and tucked at the bottom of the page a fair way in. The story had not made the front pages (yet).

The programme got scheduled airtime and the production team were all rushing about to work for the deadline a few days away. I felt grateful to the producers, runners, editors, edit studio staff, legal people, editorial people, and many others who I had no idea who they were but were doing something important around this time. The end was frenzied and because the Army said they were making arrests, the BBC put out an anonymised version of the programme so as not to prejudice any potential court case for the specific corporals. The production team were still re-watching this in the late afternoon of the 18th of September 2008 and the BBC programme was scheduled to go out at 9:00pm. BBC Broadcasting house had to have a copy of it by 8:00pm at the latest in order for it to go out on air. We didn't leave the edit studio until the last moment. A taxi was called for the production team and I to travel to hand deliver the final product. Grasping onto the master copy, we hurtled our way through the early evening London roads. There was a sense of urgency and worry about getting there in time, a sense of disbelief that we had got to this point and a sense of wonder about what would happen after it had been on TV. I had originally wanted to watch the show go out with family and friends, but as everything was so last minute the only option was to watch with the rest of the production team in the executive producer's office on the top floor of the BBC Media Centre. After everything we had gone through as a team to make it, this actually seemed like a fitting end. The master copy was in the right hands and the time came to watch.

We huddled round to watch it go out live. I had seen the footage loads of times and knew exactly what was coming, but it was somehow different knowing that it wasn't just me watching now. I could feel myself getting drawn in at the start and feeling the same feelings I had felt when I was preparing to go into the Army. I was also in slight disbelief that it was really me who had gone through all that. My phone went into melt down during the hour the BBC programme was on with messages from family and friends from past and present!

After it ended it felt like a weight had been lifted from my shoulders. Questions about 'what next' had started to creep in during this time, but I suppressed these to the bottom of my brain in order to just enjoy the moment. Critically assessing the BBC programme was far from my mind that particular evening. At that moment; I was the Undercover Soldier who had accomplished his mission.

Celebrating our own successes, however big or small have their time and place to give us a sense of positivity within systems that can minimise our feelings of individual worth and power. We can recognise our individual talents and strengths at the same time as being part of an inter-dependent collective. Resilient systems may nurture this, which in turn will contribute to a stronger and more cohesive system.

EVERY ACTION HAS A REACTION

Newton's third law of motion tells us that every action has an equal and opposite reaction. In physics, this means that when an object collides with a target, there is an equal force going into and away from the target at the same time. This can be used as a metaphor for the effects of actions we take or words we direct toward another person or target. This is inevitably going to affect how other people think and feel and how they respond back to you. Positive messages are likely to be met with reciprocated positive emotions and negative language is likely to be received and sent back the same way. Human thought and feelings are complex, so every re-action from what we say or do cannot always be predicted. Whether actions of a country at war, text in print or on social media, words on TV or in conversation, you can't take anything back once it's been said and it is out there in the ether. This doesn't mean we should not speak or act as we can't predict its consequences fully, but it means we should be aware of the power our words and actions have and consider them carefully. We also have to be prepared to react to the new situations we create.

The Undercover Soldier was seen by around 2.6 million people according to viewing figures, which along with other media coverage brought a high level of exposure to the issues. It was impossible to reflect all the light, shade and subtleties of my experiences in an hour programme on the BBC. This book is an extension of what was broadcast to illuminate the broader range of complex events and interactions. As a psychologist, I am interested in exploring the multi-faceted state of affairs and understanding the function of all the behaviours of the individuals within the context and systems they found themselves.

I was no longer undercover, but the work was not over. I had to turn up for work the next day as per usual. Everyone was waiting to see what the reaction was and what was going to happen in light of it all.

Lord Richard Dannatt had already given a recorded response to the investigation that went into the BBC programme. This served as the Army's official reaction to events. I awaited a personal response from Lord Richard Dannatt to see what the Army's response to me as an individual was.

It's been hard for me to gauge the reaction of many people on the ground within the Army because since the BBC programme went out, unsurprisingly, I haven't been in a military environment to hear people's views first hand. I have over the years picked up mixed reactions first hand from ex-soldiers and those still serving (some still at Catterick). This includes some wishing to thank me, feeling that bullying was a problem for them. It also includes those who thought it was all a waste of time and I shouldn't have done it. Some felt there were 'dodgy' things that happened, but there were still a lot of good people in the Army. Some (particularly older people) still felt young recruits 'deserved' to be beaten to help them do their job. Some seemed to respect that I had actually done six months training before commenting on the issues. Some seemed very wary of me as if they thought I may still be on the hunt for information and gave general statements that agreed with the findings in the BBC programme before turning back to their friends and bad mouthing me. I've respected all their opinions and have tried to understand how they have come to their view. In my eyes, what I did was for currently serving soldiers and recruits, so I value their opinion and if what happened has not benefitted them fully, then it's worth exploring why.

I received various texts just before, during and after the BBC programme went out on national TV. Some came from people in my platoon, people in the R platoon and from some unknown people in the Army who had got my number. There was again a real mix in reactions. Some said it was 'cool', some thanked me for what I did and wished they would have known who I was so they could have told me more stuff. Some called me a 'dick', some seemed disappointed and questioned how much of any type of friendship had been real, some asked me what I got paid to do it. I thought that was a fair set of responses. The recruits in my platoon at that time are now all in different places in their lives and in the world. Some are still in the Army, some have gone to Afghanistan, some are out the Army and some have sadly passed away. I was told I had to not speak to any of them beyond a simple text reply at this stage as the Army would be doing their own investigation into everything and anything I said may be investigated and/or interpreted in certain ways by military lawyers. Sadly, by the time the military investigation was over, someone I considered a close friend during my time in the Army had passed away in a car collision in the UK. In one of the final scenes in the BBC programme I filmed myself on the last day of the final exercise. I was in a melancholic mood and am captured saying:

> *"It's the last day of the final exercise, the last one I'll ever do in the British Army. As with the rest of them, it's been one of massive lows followed by massive highs*

over the simplest of things. You get really close to the lads in doing this. Everyone bonds really tightly and obviously they will all go off to do this for real and from time to time I'll wonder how they're doing".

I still do wonder how they are doing. Army training was an experience that develops shared bonds, even though mine were tainted.

The story appeared in most of the national papers and in many of the local Yorkshire papers. Most were simply reporting the event, who was implicated and what was happening as a result. Some of the stories weren't quite from the angle the production team and I had expected.

One of the most talked about articles and one I *really* hadn't expected appeared on the front of the Sun Newspaper on the 20th of September 2008. The headline simply read:

You're *in* the Army now

The strap-line following this up read:

'A BBC reporter who joined the Army to expose bullying may be sent to war, it emerged yesterday.'

'WHAT!' echoed loudly in my head as I reached for the phone to call the BBC legal team!

It turned out this wasn't really going to happen, but it was a sensational headline. I had been officially discharged from the Army and was protected by the BBC. Still, it was worrying for family and friends. During my time in training I realised that the Sun was the paper of choice among squaddies at Catterick. I knew many would read and accept the Sun's slant on what had happened and the investigation may lose its worth in changing the training culture in the Army at the very place where there was the scope for real improvement. That saddened me, but felt unable to do anything about it at that stage and resigned to continue to watch the political theatre. The Sun approached the BBC for a response to their story but didn't see fit to include it in their piece and unfortunately also got details of the investigation wrong. The BBC response was as follows:

> *'We would never comment on a hypothetical situation but the MoD will no doubt want to focus on the issues raised by the programme rather than the individual who helped raise them. We are cooperating with the Army in their investigations'.*

Different papers reported different aspects of the BBC programme and different allegations. Many focused on the Corporals who were facing court and the number of allegations against them. Most led with the facts at the time which were:

> *'Five army training instructors have been suspended after fresh allegations of bullying at the Army's biggest training base, at Catterick in North Yorkshire.*

The instructors, all corporals, were alleged to have punched, kicked, shaken, throttled, and urinated on trainee infantry and rifle recruits at the base. The alleged abuse was revealed by an undercover reporter for the BBC. The government has pledged to crack down on the bullying of recruits following the scandal at Deepcut in Surrey, where four teenage soldiers died amid allegations of bullying and harassment.' (Matthew Weaver, The Guardian, 19th September 2008)

The Guardian also gave differing points of view from different people with different stakes in this investigation that I found interesting:

- General Sir Richard Dannatt said: "The army does not allow bullying in any shape or form. There will always be some who get it wrong - my aim is to reduce it to an absolute minimum."
- The Ministry of Defence added: "We were already in the process of investigating several of the cases highlighted by the BBC."
- Kevan Jones, a Labour member of the defence select committee, said: "There needs to be an independent body with teeth, away from the chain of command. Unless you have that mechanism this sort of thing will continue to happen."
- Lynn Farr, whose 18-year-old son, Daniel, died while training at the barracks in 1997, said the army needed to prove it had zero tolerance of bullying. "It's good that this film has highlighted what we have been screaming about for years,

and what the MoD has been denying," she said. Farr, who set up a campaign to combat bullying in the army, said she was still contacted by recruits with allegations of abuses. "I'm more saddened than shocked. Things have improved at Catterick but there is still a problem."

- Liberal Democrat shadow Defence Secretary Nick Harvey said that the latest claims of bullying were proof that the Army had failed to eradicate it despite a zero tolerance policy.

It was even discussed on Newswatch in which Ian Tandy (a PR spokesperson who has previously served in the Army) opposed the programme for several reasons. One criticism of the programme was that most of it was footage of recruits saying what had happened to them and might not be a fair reflection of reality as it was hearsay. I couldn't be invisible to film on the rifle ranges, have a camera attached to my helmet as I crawled through the mud over the moors or be hidden in a toilet bowl in another platoon's building ready to pop up when a corporal beat them. Filming recruits saying what had happened to them and what they had seen was how the investigation had to be done. I believed the experiences that I didn't see for myself were real for recruits and they had no reason to make things up when they spoke to me as they didn't know I was undercover. I also verified incidents with other witnesses. Catterick Garrison is a large place with a lot going on. I randomly happened to be placed within a certain platoon by the Army, meaning I would get to know this platoon extremely well and due to the nature of training it would be difficult (but not impossible) to have access to other platoons and places in the training barracks. If I had been in another platoon and in the right place at the right time to record footage of a beating, seeing an incident of abuse on screen would have made it more difficult for some to disregard and diminish important testimony of recruits.

It was a mix of emotions seeing the story and my face spread across the national and local media. I was partially glad people were taking note and that papers were (mostly) accurately reporting allegations and possible ramifications from the investigation, but still concerned about the amount of negativity online and in some newspapers. The actions of the BBC, the MOD and of me had resulted in several re-actions and these would continue to drive a lot further actions for some time to come.

Awareness that our words and actions have consequences is vital. Although they may not always have the consequences we intended, if our awareness continues, we can still shape our reactions along with others. Sometimes it may be that we choose to view a situation in a different manner and, as a result, it has a different impact on lives.

6:

THE RE-ORGANISATION

"Every area of trouble gives out a ray of hope; and the one unchangeable certainty is that nothing is certain or unchangeable"

- John F Kennedy, 35th President of the United States

NEGOTIATING SOCIAL MEDIA AND SOCIAL COMPARISON

There are many benefits to our increasingly developed technology and use of the internet and social media such as being more easily connected and able to share or access positive interactions, relationships and resources. It can be a good source of social action, individual expression and raising awareness. To make the most of these benefits, social media needs to be used safely. It can result in too much social comparison where people present idealised versions of their life that we feel we need to live up to or compete with and this can cause anxiety and insecurity. Those with existing low self-esteem can use social media to post pictures or information presenting themselves in an idealised way to others or to seek attention, but may in turn contribute to the web of intoxicating social comparison and have the adverse effect on their esteem by leaving themselves open to negative comments and reactions. Cyber-bullying or 'trolling' is becoming more common and extreme in language. When using social media it is easy to detach yourself from thinking about the target of your language as a real human. People can also access your personal photos if you don't have the right privacy settings. Social media isn't something to be scared of and can be really helpful for our connections, self-expression and resilience if used thoughtfully and alongside real life interactions.

Certain groups used Facebook as a forum to rally together and express their displeasure at the BBC, the BBC programme and at me. It is more common today to see social media used as a tool for social action and people are more aware of social media privacy and abuse issues.

At the time, it was a relatively new phenomena and this may have been one of the first cases where Facebook was used in this way. On the social media website there was a petition to send me to Afghanistan, some groups calling me a 'gimp' and several other more undignified words that I'll leave to your imagination. There were also links to BBC complaint websites. One Facebook group that has now been taken off had at one point over 11,000 members. Others groups I noted on November 3rd, 2008 included:

- Russell Sharp Is a Complete Gimp and should be sent to the front line

(3888 members)

- Bring that twat who made under cover soldier to justice [sic] arrested for treason

(961 members)

- Rusell Sharp [sic] "Undercover Soldier" should be tried for treason

(5110 members)

- send undercover soldier (russel sharp[sic]) to report in afgan

(1,143 members)

I expected and accepted some negative reaction and knew that having gone against a prevailing culture in the Army where 'snitching' is discouraged, I was automatically going to receive a defensive response as that group tried to maintain itself. I could also understand the disappointment of my training staff that spent time training me and my fellow recruits. The use of social media in this way had surprised me at the time and whether you (or I) feel I 'deserved' it or not, it was difficult to read as I felt I had good intentions going into the project and (maybe naively) felt this would be reflected in a way that would lessen some of the negative feelings from others. Some posts did separate me from the BBC which helped and were generally less scathing, but many targeted me directly as the face of the operation.

The BBC had thought to protect me at the time by contacting Facebook and having them taken straight down, but it was thought that by doing this it would instigate people to form other groups and provoke a stronger reaction. It was deemed the best course of action by the BBC to let the groups continue and quietly remove them when things died down. These Facebook groups were still around until 2011 when most were removed, although there are still remnants floating about today.

Part of me was grateful for the positive comments and was amused that my name was now enshrined in Wikipedia. The other part of me was reeling from the many negative comments thrown at my name and some threats on internet forums of violence against me. This left me feeling paranoid for a couple of weeks after and nervous of cars stopping near me at night if I was walking about. Fortunately, I was in Leeds during this time and felt comfort that I was around friends and I knew the geography well of all the little rabbit warrens to weave in and out of to avoid suspect cars or people. One evening, I had left a small gathering at a friend's house that was only a ten minute walk from where I was living. It was dark and slightly foggy and I was by myself. I saw a long black car drive slowly past me and then make some unnatural moves involving braking and turning in the road. I couldn't see into the car, but I didn't want to either. I crossed the road and stepped over a wall to take an alternative route across a field so I didn't have to go past the car. The car was moving slowly but no one got out. I kept an eye out behind me but the car eventually moved off when I had got too far away. I wondered who it was. It turned out it was another friend of mine who was driving a new car and he was going to offer me a lift back. He said he thought he had freaked me out and understood why I took off without me saying anything. This time period was uncomfortable and I stopped reading online forums because of it. I felt like I was running, but I shouldn't be. I started to realise I should be fighting (in the metaphorical sense), facing issues head on and living life out in the open in the hope those with an interest in the Media, the Army or life in general could learn something from what had happened.

I was asked to attend a question and answer session internally at the BBC for an editorial policy meeting. The room was full of 'important' people at the BBC (i.e. they had grand job titles and some power in programme making terms). I didn't feel daunted at being surrounded by these people as I knew no-one had experienced what I had and so decided just to talk from the heart. I just enjoyed getting my story out to people there who knew what it took to make a programme and how difficult the process was. It was commented that I was 'amongst friends' on this occasion, and it did feel that way. I had several people come up to me after and wish me well.

I got noticed a few times on the street in the days after the BBC programme aired. It is a strange feeling when people recognise you, but you have no idea who they are. I got asked for a picture on a shopping street in Ealing, London by a middle aged woman. I obliged the picture, but didn't stop to talk as I wasn't really sure whether it was a good idea or not. As she was being pleasant, I didn't want to be rude. I received quite a few looks of recognition walking around London in the few days after the BBC programme. However, at times I couldn't tell if they were looking at me because they recognised me or my own vanity was making me look around more to see if people recognised me and that was making people look back to see who was staring at them, even though they didn't recognise me! On one occasion I was stood on the tube heading towards central London on a busy rush hour. It was crammed as you would expect. I was stood right behind a guy who was reading about me in the paper. I was just behind him, out of his line of sight and could read the paper over his left shoulder. He was reading the story and there was a nice big picture of me on the page. He never turned around and saw me, but I laughed to myself at the thought of how incredibly unlikely it is that you read about someone you have never met in the paper and they are stood right next to you. I toyed with freaking him out. I was going to ask him if I could read the article and just hold the paper so he could see me and the picture together and wait until he noticed. I even thought of ducking down under the paper and standing up quickly so my head burst right through the picture in the paper and it would be like I had come to life! I decided to leave it alone and let a happy coincidence go unnoticed. Apart from being totally stupid, another reason I left it alone is that I just didn't know if his reaction toward me would be positive, negative or indifferent. I was reticent to speak to unknown people about it in case their reaction was as negative as the comments online had been. A story that exemplifies this was highlighted in Marks and Spencer's in Harrogate, three days after the BBC programme. My paranoia was already a little heightened by the fact that Harrogate has a training centre for younger recruits there. I wasn't sure who I may bump into. While I was wandering around the men's suits section I heard a male voice come from beside me and out the corner of my left eye I saw what seemed to be a tall, burley male looming towards me. The voice said "Here, are you the undercover soldier". My first reaction was to look up innocently and say "no" while looking slightly puzzled! When the panic subsided and I focused on the male, I saw that although he was tall and stocky, he wasn't very old and wasn't looking particularly menacing. I had already set the tone by saying I wasn't the undercover solider though. The young man, said "are you sure, you look like him and he is supposed to be from around this part of the world". As I'd already said "no" and still didn't know his true intentions I embarked on a road of duel identity that came so naturally having been undercover for so long. I said that someone else had said I looked like him, but that I wasn't. The young man wasn't fully taken in and said, "well I don't know if you are him and you just don't want to say, but I thought the programme was really good". Although I finally knew his intentions were positive in speaking to me, I had already gone down the road that I wasn't the undercover solider and didn't want to backtrack now. I continued to look confused until he went away. I felt bad though as he was obviously very observant.

Shortly after, I met up with one of my closest friends for dinner that I hadn't seen since the BBC programme aired. When we sat down to the table he made a comment that intrigued me. He said, "funny, it doesn't feel like I'm having dinner with a celebrity yet". I wondered how symbolic this was of people's perceptions of what a 'celebrity' was. If I was vaguely on some celebrity list for the week after the BBC programme aired, I'm definitely well off the list now. Time moves on and news stories become old and as quickly as fame comes, it can go just the same. I thought that those who gained celebrity and wanted to keep it would have to act in certain ways to maintain that status. This would be driven by public perceptions and organisations that are benefiting from that person being a 'celebrity' and not by what you may choose to do independently. It didn't feel like this would be the right motivation in life to drive your actions and achieve your goals in a way that kept you comfortable with your own values and having the freedom to act independently. I was glad to have tasted some 'fame', but equally glad to realise it doesn't have to change you. Especially if becoming briefly 'famous' is only a by-product of what you are actually focusing on doing in your life and not the reason for your action in the first place. There are deep rooted psychological reasons why we as humans seek 'fame' and promote ourselves on social media, including evolutionary, social and personal meaning making factors related to our anxiety about our fragile mortality and need to be accepted, belong and recognised as unique. In the modern world this is exacerbated by systems such as capitalism that support commodification of our selves. Increased social recognition or 'status' and having increased perceived social influence, power and wealth can also contribute to us chasing fame to meet our underlying psychological needs. It is a powerful influence on what we think will make us happy in the modern world, but to be truly resilient and have a better overall wellbeing we need to recognise our psychological frailty in this area and seek to meet our needs around esteem and belonging and making sense of our mortality in alternative and more long-lasting positive ways.

RESTORATION OF RELATIONSHIPS AND RESOURCES

Restorative practices are important for our own mental health and resilience. Making sure we have the correct mental or physical resources restored if they are depleted can help us be ready to continue to face life and anything else that may come our way. As positive relationships are so important to our wellbeing, it's vital that if these have been affected, they need to be restored as well. We have all had the feeling of having a difficult conversation with someone and then leaving this hanging in the air for so long that it weighs on our mind and is very uncomfortable to be around that person and address the issue. It can be hard to take the first step to try and open a conversation when there has been difficulty, but life is short and in not doing so it may end up being something that we regret. Community Police can use restorative practice to allow victims and offenders to meet and share and understand how each other was feeling during an incident. This can help both parties at least come to terms with what has happened. Restorative conversations are increasingly being used in education too to support positive relationships between peers and between teachers and young people to allow all to be in a place where they are ready to learn and feel safe and supported.

When reorganising after a battle, soldiers need to check what ammunition is left and restore it to full. Following the investigation the Army needed to restore some order through a military investigation. The BBC production team and I helped with this restoration by cooperating with the investigation and I hoped this may also restore some of the relationships between the two organisations and myself as well.

Up until this moment I wasn't sure what response the Army would legally try to take towards me. I received a letter personally addressed to me from General Sir Richard Dannatt (now Lord Dannatt). There were four main points in the letter.

1. They were disappointed that I hadn't told anyone of senior rank about incidents I became aware of when I was actually in the Army.

2. They said they could take me to court and I could face up to three months in jail for swearing allegiance to the Queen under false pretences...

3. ...but they didn't see that it was appropriate to do so as the BBC and I were now fully co-operating and helping with the military investigation.

4. They were pleased for the donation of all my earnings while in the Army to Help for Heroes fund.

Point one didn't really make sense as this would have negated the whole reason for me being there in the first place. Point two was worrying, but I drew a sigh of relief at point three. My personal aim was to help and not attack the Army, so I was glad they accepted (if they didn't really appreciate) the co-operation. I was also thankful to the BBC legal team who kept me safe on this front and who had assured me they would back me and that there were strong legal grounds for all we did. Point four was good to hear and something that wasn't publicised in the papers. I often get asked what happened to the money that the Army paid me and I think some people assume I kept it. All my salary received from the Army as a recruit for six months was held in a separate bank account and was sent to Help for Heroes fund. This amounted to well over £5,000. Hopefully this will have gone towards good charity work.

The Military checked its own ammunition and went in search for evidence of the claims of wrongdoing. This included investigations into K platoon and R platoon in particular. Investigations took a long time and I had to be on standby at any point to answer questions. We also gave the Military police access to everything the team and I had recorded or made notes of in regard to the project. There was days-worth of footage when put all together and piles of notes and correspondence. It wasn't until the end of 2008 when I was interviewed by a member of the Special Investigation Branch Royal Military Police.

I was nervous about meeting him and I got a vague sense that he had similar feelings due to my reputation for secret filming! However, conversation and exchange was friendly. The Captain presented a list of questions he had compiled about the footage and/or notes. Most of the questions just involved clarifying who said what and who was where at what time etc. I was happy to go through all this with him and it was a bit of a trip down memory lane for me. It took most of one whole day to go through all this. The next time we met he took statements down for things I had witnessed with a view for using it as evidence in court. I described incidents he asked me about and gave my account of what I had seen. He took good notes and wrote up my statement there and then for me to sign.

I enjoyed talking to the Captain about some of the lads I knew and whom he now knew from interviewing them. It was good to have updated information about how they were doing and where they were. The Captain told me that they had found some more problems and issues within the two platoons than had been mentioned in the BBC programme. He wouldn't say what these were at the time so as not to jeopardise any court case. His view was that some of the allegations (at the time) were serious, but in the grand scheme of things others were not. This resonated with what I had experienced and he had independently backed up my thoughts about what I had witnessed in context.

The Captain also spoke of an R recruit who had died in Afghanistan since training. I had heard of this recruit but never spoke to him personally. The Captain said it here to attempt to give some perspective of the issues the platoon members faced as well as dealing with the ongoing military investigations. The Captain gave his view of bullying in the Army in general; he believed that no-one would ever stop bullying totally in the Army, but what we could do was to help reduce it slowly and make people think before they acted. This felt like a fair viewpoint and resonated with me.

One other interesting point that arose from a discussion with the Captain was when he told us that recruitment for the Infantry had gone up in Middlesbrough, just after the BBC programme was broadcast. I wasn't sure if this was true or not, how much a rise in recruitment could be directly linked to the BBC programme, or how I felt about this if it was true. The Captain said in Middlesbrough (at the time) they asked prospective recruits if they had seen the BBC programme. Those who had seen it would apparently say that Army training didn't look as bad as they had thought and they had almost expected training to be 'Full Metal Jacket' style. As I mentioned, watching Full Metal Jacket before embarking on Army training is not a good idea and I hope my stories in this book have provided a more realistic account of training experiences.

The investigations went on for over six months after the BBC programme before it was addressed in Parliament. As part of her response to the Armed Forces Complaint Commissioner's first annual report, Joan Humble MP asked on 22 of April 2009, what progress had been made in the investigation of allegations of physical abuse and harassment at Catterick Barracks.

Mr. Kevan Jones gave the reply that;

> *"we were already aware of some of the allegations made by the BBC in its 'The Undercover Soldier' documentary in September [2008]. A Royal Military Police (Special Investigation Branch) investigation had been initiated in February [2008]. For those we were not aware of, an RMP(SIB) investigation was launched as soon as the BBC made us aware of their concerns. These investigations are continuing."*

Relationships and resources can take a long time to restore and it can be an uncomfortable process. It is vital to engage with to re-affirm positive connections, re-build stronger understanding and support our resilient social functioning as an individual, a group or a system.

LETTING GO AND MOVING ON

We all have to deal with 'loss' at some point in our lives whether this be through the death of a loved one, loss of a treasured object, or a change in situation or circumstance. There can be many factors that hinder us accepting or coming to terms with significant challenging events or loss. To be resilient we need to find ways to manage our emotions so we can continue to function well in our lives. There are many ways in which this can happen and the process and time frame for doing so can be as unique as the individual going through it. This may ultimately involve some form of acceptance, management of a range of different thoughts and emotions and development of some ways to safely identify with both the past and the present in a way that is meaningful.

There have been many deaths reported of UK soldiers in Afghanistan – Helmand province in particular and most notably in the summer of 2009. The number of casualties is never fully reported but I'm sure this would be a terrifying statistic. It's easy to almost desensitise yourself to it as it has been such a regular occurrence over the last decade and to forget the real life impact this has on the friends and families lives of those soldiers. British force deaths from the war in Afghanistan stands at 454 from October 2001 to July 2015. Over 2,110 were admitted to hospital for being wounded in action from hostile conflict between January 2006 and March 2013. This shows the toughness and the reality of job. In order to have the best chance of survival and operate as a successful unit, every man needs to be skilled, aware of others and have good attention to detail in their tactics and actions. Their survival and that of their comrades depend on it. It can be easy to take the view that specific incidents of 'bullying' are low level and don't matter within this big picture, but it may be that these little pieces of the jigsaw contribute to the whole. The smaller scale incidents can help us generate discourse on the whole of Army training itself and question if it is as efficient as it could be. It helps us question why incidents related to bullying may have more wide reaching consequences than just its physical effects in terms how effectively recruits actually learn and apply their learning. This learning and application of it is imperative to increasing survival in the harsh conditions. For me, this was the discourse worth having from the undercover investigation that was never quite openly achieved; the discourse over and above the individual cases of incidents related to bullying.

The court cases were hampered for many reasons. It meant I couldn't draw a line under this chapter or 'move on' until both court cases were finished. The same was also true for any of the involved training staff or recruits. This left us all in limbo. This was the case for almost two years after the BBC programme.

This gave me time to reflect on what we had done and how we had done it. It gave me an opportunity to process the events, the change and consider the future. Part of me was still held by the significant experience so it made throwing myself fully into anything new was challenging for many years.

We all need time to process significant events in our lives and loss. It is normal to go through a range of emotions such as anger, denial, sadness, guilt, fear and for these to affect you physically and emotionally. As you assimilate to the new situation it is important to use resources such as time and family and friends or other support networks to think about and talk about your feelings to make sense of them. It is better to face your feelings than suppress them and having a creative outlet can help. Looking after yourself is important as well as not having any expectations of how you should or shouldn't be feeling. Accepting your loss and your new situation and feeling 'ok' again is not the same as forgetting. In fact, the memories of the past can become more and more integral to defining the people we are and the future paths we take.

VALUES AND THEIR INFLUENCE

Values can be thought of as abstract ideals. There may also be values that we share innately, regardless of their linguistic expression, as they are important for our universal psychological motivations around surviving life. Values are mental processes that combine cognitive representations such as concepts, goals, and beliefs with emotional attitudes that have positive or negative valence. Goals need not be arbitrary wants, but can derive from fundamental human needs, including both biological needs such as food, water, and shelter, and psychological needs for relatedness, competence, and autonomy[19].

The values we hold can drive our present day actions and our hopes for the future. When I was an employee of both the BBC and the MOD, both organisations had

---

19 Richard M. Ryan and Edward L. Deci (2000) Intrinsic and Extrinsic Motivations: Classic Definitions and New Directions. Contemporary Educational Psychology 25, 54–67.

a duty of care to me. In return, as an employee, I had a duty to conduct myself in a manner that reflected the organisations core values. It's interesting to note that the core values of both organisation on their websites have changed over the last decade. This shows that values are not fixed. There is quite a lot of commonality between most values of large public sector organisations and are typically around being open and honest with integrity and respecting the interests or views of others. These values can sound like 'management speak', but can also be a core vision that tries to drive a positive service of the organisation.

One of my favourite paradigms that kept coming into my head as I was on this journey as the undercover solider was:

Which is mightier, the pen or the sword?

What is mightier, the written guidelines and law against bullying or the physical strength of the bully, the journalist or the infantry man, the BBC or the MOD?

I was fully trained by both organisations. I felt like a metaphysical walking version of the paradigm amongst the elite educated journalists who use their pen to fight their trade and the hardest soldiers who have killed and experienced war. Like most debates in the same vain, the 'answer' is almost always 'both'- or at least an appreciation of both serving a purpose at a different moment in time and place. I respected the best of both sides immensely as I walked amongst them. You could recognise 'the best' in each organisation and I reflected on what made them stand out. I felt it was not only the display of the mastery of their chosen skill set, but that their manner and demeanour showed a clear connection between their organisation's core values and their personal values. Their actions in life and in their job were seemingly joined by the same driving principles and they transcended themselves, fairly helping and supporting others in the most effective manner in their context.

Hang on a moment, who the hell am I to get on my high horse about values? I'm a two faced, deceptive, secret filming, lying little toad aren't I? I have to acknowledge that even though I had positive intentions in my mind and attempted to be true to them supporting the public interest, I did deceive several people. This puts me in a position of being a bit of a hypocrite.

This hypocritical dilemma of 'if two wrongs ever make a right' was questioned in a similar context in one of Derren Brown's special shows on Channel 4 where he put a member of the public undercover ('Miracles for Sale' which aired on 25th April, 2011). This was to investigate the reality behind the faith healing phenomenon in America and the belief in faith-inspiring miraculous recoveries. Specifically, it was to highlight those who fake such things to obtain money from those in vulnerable situations. The person going undercover had to adopt the guise of a pastor and miracle worker in order to mix in their circles. I found it interesting that they showed moments Derren Brown's team were in moral conflict and thought it was very humbling and humanising, if not a little uncomfortable to watch. They had to decide if it was worth a faith healer being disgraced, face losing their income, reputation, and causing their family to potentially struggle all in the name of 'truth.' This resonated with my experience. They straddled the conflict between the exploitation of the many (believers) and of the few (healers). I doubt that it was planned that this would be in the programme when they first started the project, but was something they reacted to when filming. Rather than hide this discussion in the edit suite never to be talked about in case it jeopardised their programme, they laid it all out on the table. In doing this it brought us along as an audience and emphasised their core values for partaking in such a project. It was open and reflective and even showed moments of direct conflict between the undercover reporter and the production team. When the person going undercover questioned if his wrong made a right, they went on a short journey to explore why people do such things. The conclusion they came to on that journey to proceed with the project was that 'we must be hypocrites sometimes to expose the true reality'.

Regular reflection on our core values at a personal and organisational level and can help guide us on a journey of moral and ethical uncertainty in a complex social world.

UNDERSTANDING OUR SEARCH FOR MEANING

There are psychological models[20] that suggest humans have an innate mechanism for 'making meaning' in their lives. This is a 'need' to make relational sense of our own mortality, our self- esteem, our feeling of certainty and our sense of belonging. There may be other core needs as well. If we aren't able to make meaning in one of the areas, we look to focus on other areas where we can make meaning.

20 Heine, S., Proulx, T., Vohs, K (2006) The Meaning Maintenance Model: On the Coherence of Social Motivations. Personality and Social Psychology Review. 1 (2) 88-100).

When our ability to make meaning in many of the areas is violated it can lead to increased anxiety and this over time can result in negative feelings such as depression. Much of this is unconscious and subtle, but it affects our mood and our behaviour as we try to regain a sense of meaningfulness in the areas we need to. This can leave us vulnerable to getting involved in activities that may not be the most helpful for us long-term, but meet our needs at the time (i.e. joining a gang involved in crime if we don't feel we 'belong' anywhere else and they make us feel 'valued').

Following the BBC programme, I was given a year contract to work within various BBC departments. This length of contract was rare at the time and even rarer now. Contracts are now generally very short and fit for purpose. When I was first approached by the BBC to become the Undercover Soldier, the executive producer at the time told me that I may be in some psychological turmoil about what to 'do next' after being in such an extreme and involving project. His words rang true now I was at this point. It wasn't that I needed to try find another 'buzz' from being involved in intense high-profile project (after all the hard physical work and double life, I was looking forward to something easier going and low key), but I had uncomfortable feelings of being unsure where my skills as an undercover reporter could be transferred to and what I actually wanted to do. As I had done the job at a high level, I didn't have any aspiration to do this exact type of work again straight away. I thought I could link to my experience in psychology or with education. I was pushed by some to know what I wanted to do and to get myself 'out there' amongst BBC members with a bit of media clout while my name was still resonating around the building. This relied on my motivation to be high, but at this time it was not. There were psychological effects on myself from being involved in the intense undercover project that I hadn't appreciated.

While I was making my mind up about what avenue to explore working in, I was placed in 'science development'. They are responsible for coming up with ideas for science documentaries, developing these ideas and pitching them to executives in order to get them commissioned for a production team to make and then broadcast. I would see how programmes were initially conceived and developed. It was my first day with them and I felt as everyone feels on their first day in a new job, but with the additional complexity of still processing the undercover programme and its aftermath. I saw my phone ringing and that it was my uncle. I had seen him a couple of days before at my Grandfather's eightieth birthday in Leeds. I went over to a window that overlooked the surrounding urban sprawl near the desk I had been given to work at. I had one of those feelings when I saw my uncle ringing that could be mistaken for psychic ability. I put together the fact that my Grandfather hadn't looked healthy when I saw him and my uncle ringing at an unexpected time and felt something bad had happened. He told me my Grandfather had died of a heart attack. After he told me I stared out the window for a good few minutes trying to keep myself composed. Part of me tried to cope with the loss by thinking that if you're going to go, reaching eighty and having a party with all your family and friends just before is a pretty good way for it to happen. This didn't change the fact that his life had ended. I turned to look back inside the media building and it all didn't seem to make sense anymore. I went to my new boss and managed to speak to say I would like to go home even though it was my first day and told my old production team (who were working in a different part of the building and wondering how my first day was going) that I was going home. I left the BBC building and went to the tube station. Instead of actually getting the tube I slumped into one of the seats on the platform and stared. Stared into air as people busily walked past me, stared as the trains pulled into the station and pulled out again, stared as the announcements came over the speaker.

I sat there for a long time while everything flashed past me. I don't know how long. It felt like my body had become incapacitated and my mind was the only working organ, replaying parts of my life in a kaleidoscopic pattern. I think my grandfather's death also brought back a lot of memories from my fathers' passing and the end of his life. The last decade of my father's life was marred by Multiple Sclerosis. I remember on the day my father had died and I had said my tearful goodbyes over his still body for the last time, I came out of the room and put my arms around my grandfather telling him that dad had been a soldier. Of course, I didn't know what it was like to be a soldier then, but he had fought on like one. You could even call him an undercover soldier, as due to the degenerative effects of the type of Multiple Sclerosis he had, he couldn't speak for the last three years of his life. From my slump on the platform everything got on top of me and I questioned everything I was doing and had done. The loneliness of a new life in London was emphasised by over a year in some form of undercover situation with no proper social relations. I had no real direction for what I wanted to do in my future. I was far from family and friends and in no close relationship with anyone. I couldn't work out if I was celebrated for my efforts undercover or if I had become one of the most despised men in Britain at the time. I questioned if the last year had all been pointless. I wondered what sort of name I had given to the Sharp family and what I wanted it to stand for now I was carrying the name on from my father's and grandfather's death. Everything seemed meaningless as objects continued past my glazed eyes in a dark blur and my emotionless face felt like it was floating in slow motion above my body.

Relating back to the model of meaning making, I struggled to make meaning about:

- My public perception and my reputation that would live on after my physical form deceased

(Symbolic immortality need)

- My sense of belonging in a new city where I didn't know many people

(Affiliation need)

- My esteem when I couldn't use the skills I had developed and had to try new things again

(Self-esteem need)

- My uncertain future occupation and life I was heading towards with few feelings of control

(Certainty need)

An unknown amount of time later, I eventually felt able to move and managed to drag myself back to my flat. This was the start of a real downward spiral for my sense of well-being. My psychological state was always monitored by the production team (and myself) over the actual period I was undercover in the Army. Despite a few dips over the Christmas period, I seemed to manage being undercover with relatively emotional and physical ease. It was when it was over that cracks started to appear. Despite seemingly having a lot going for me at the time and potential opportunities that people spend years trying to get, I found it revealing that my state of mind did not match up to this. What I craved at this particular time was friends close by, a genuine sense of purpose and a genuine sense of belonging.

The people in science development were very patient with me. I carried on trying to work because I wanted to appear useful. I worked for three weeks on developing a psychological documentary before being put to work on random bits and pieces until I found a project to work on. I found it a real struggle to concentrate and I constantly felt tired. I genuinely thought I had got less intelligent as I couldn't seem to think as quickly as I used to. During brainstorming sessions I felt like I had no imagination and if I had to write anything it took me a long time to create one sentence before my concentration went and I had to go for a walk before I did another sentence. My emotional part of by brain (limbic system) was being used too much, preventing my cortex from being able to function efficiently. This happens to us all when we have too many feelings to manage. My low productivity and motivation carried on for months, but (perhaps related to Army training) I found some way to keep going. I decided to take up an opportunity to see an independent counsellor that I had been offered on completion of the project, but had previously turned down. It was helpful to have a 'sounding board' with someone who was removed from the job situation and my personal life so I didn't feel I had to hide any particular thoughts and feelings. Discussion about why I may find it hard to concentrate if I am processing so many things helped, as well as exercises to improve focus. The suggestion of exercise being important also helped and I would walk home after every day and joined a basketball team in London. I think ultimately, the independent discussion helped me solidify feelings I already had about how to pull myself out of this hole, make sense of my thoughts and spur me on to actually do something about it. Time passed and I had started to naturally build a friendship base in London as well as Leeds and had got my bearings with new ways of working.

There were also some side effects from leaving the Army and returning to a life without the same routine and discipline. I had physical withdrawal symptoms from using my body so much in the Army and then going straight to being sat in offices. I can only describe this as my muscles craving to be moved and used, full of trapped energy waiting to explode. I also had to wait on court cases and military investigations and to know if I would have to be called as a witness. I couldn't let my head slip too far from everything that happened in case my memory came in to question by the defence. I think I've now lost most of the habits and drills I picked up during Army training. Some say this is a bad thing as I don't iron or make my bed as well anymore! The only long standing effect is when I am in a forest area or English moor, I do still look across the land and think of where to camouflage myself, what to look for and where to take cover if I was shot at! I don't think this is a bad thing though and you never know when it might save a life! I also had a strong urge to do paintballing for many years after the Army!

Around March 2009 I started to pull my life back together and felt the best I had since the BBC programme had gone out in September 2008. Although this time was uncomfortable, I think it was a time that made me a stronger person for having gone through it. My resilience had been developed from some adversity and I felt not only a recovery, but a personal growth about how I may go about life and what was important to focus on.

I was starting to feel more productive and took on more work at the BBC. On one occasion back in science development, we took a trip to a book store in London to look around for inspiration for potential new science documentaries. I felt invigorated by the process and came up with several ideas. One I was particularly proud of was about the science of 'shapes' in our world. Links between shapes of galaxies, to planets, to land features, to humans, to bacteria. Although I wasn't credited for it (and didn't expect to be), I'm pretty certain this idea later turned into episode 2 of 'The Code' presented by Marcus de Sautoy on BBC 1 on Aug 3rd 2011 at 9pm. The idea had been developed since conception, but still included the same content, questions and even presenter that I had suggested. It was interesting to see the length some things take as it was almost two and a half years from the seeds of an idea to having something realised on TV. The BBC thrives on creative ideas, although these can go through several people and will ultimately end up shaped by those at the top to suit a corporate purpose.

I met a lot of very creative people in the various development departments at the BBC. It was a hive of activity and I think to be part of it for some time was reward enough. A lot of the work I saw being attempted justified the licence fee to me and I doubt many other groups of people could research, create, produce and broadcast some of the epic documentaries the BBC produce. It amused me that in BBC buildings people constantly walk past each other and might make judgements about who they see based on their current job title or the way they are dressed (as we all do initially); but then you find out the fascinating things they have worked on, places they have been and things they have done and it alters your perception. We all walk past people with valuable experiences everyday but don't realise it, unless we take the time to stop and talk to each other and appreciate all our combined stories.

A boost to our sense of meaningfulness is when we can link past experiences and skills we have previously learned and developed to the present in a way that feels like what we have done in our life has some relevance and purpose. I was asked to go undercover again as a protester for a potential Panorama programme on the G20 summit in London in 2009.

The G20 summit has become notorious for the death of Ian Tomlinson and the police handling of the whole affair. Along with a colleague, I got some quite unique footage of some protesters clashes and the banks being broken into and police handling of the crowd, but wasn't near the spot where Ian Tomlinson was pushed over that day. The majority of the protest had an atmosphere of peaceful protesting and an almost carnival like mood. There were a few groups of protesters who were obviously there to cause trouble and along with a colleague we followed some youths covered in black who barged their way through police cordons early on. The atmosphere turned very tense in areas. With regard to the police handling that day, which has been widely discussed due to the case of Ian Tomlinson, I have to say that I did feel myself being filled with animosity towards the police when I was in role as a 'protester'. There was one occasion when a line of police had asked a group of protesters to move that I was stood with. I turned away and walked slowly with my hand in my pockets responding to their request. I posed no threat at all, yet one police man pushed me hard in my back. I stayed on my feet but did suddenly turn and look at him with distain. I did feel some of the police on this occasion did stir up more trouble because of their handling of the crowd. I don't know whether the policeman who pushed me felt scared, was full of testosterone, had a bad day or what, but I was walking away and was posing no threat whatsoever. My main job on that day really was to keep my colleague safe. We stuck together most of the time, but on the odd occasion we were herded by the police in different directions and we lost each other slightly. During one incidence of this, my colleague took the initiative to stand up high near one of the banks that was being smashed up in order to get good footage with a small handheld camera.

I kept my eye on him, but the crowd started to turn and I felt myself getting moved further away. At that moment I saw a glass bottle in my peripheral vision flying towards him. A large man moved into my line of vision as the bottle approached. I heard the bottle smash and I could see the glass explode outwards, but I couldn't see my colleague. For that brief second my brain filled in the missing information in my visual field. I pictured my colleague with his head cut open and blood pouring everywhere. As I pushed the man to the side and looked ahead with wide eyes expecting the worst, I saw the bottle had smashed just above his head on the wall and although he had glass remains on his shoulders, he was fine. He looked a little stunned, but then just carried on filming like it was nothing. It made me think that we were both out there putting ourselves in danger on behalf of the BBC and I did wonder if this sort of thing was really worth it. The whole place was a bit like a media circus. Every incident, every sight of blood and the world's media was jumping all over each other to get the best footage. While I was sometimes caught up in that 'excitement' to get the footage, on other occasions I did wonder what drove us all to put ourselves in these stupid and dangerous situations. I suppose different people had different motivations.

Shortly after this I secured a job working on Rogue Traders. I was taken on to do background research to get good stories to go on the programme. I got to sit with the Watchdog team at the time who were talented individuals and all worked very hard with quick turnaround times for programmes. I spent six weeks on Rogue Traders looking for unhygenic restaurants or cafes that we could potentially put someone undercover in. I had to ring many environmental and health agencies to see if I could get any leads on unhygienic places and do my own research background investigations. I went on a few field trips to cafes I had identified to see if it was as bad as it potentially sounded and if I could suss out how to get someone undercover there if so. I enjoyed the work for a while and I could see that the production team were willing to give me more training and make me part of the team full time. However, I realised that I was in danger of being too specialised and typecast in this area and I would be stuck in undercover investigations for any career I may have wanted with the BBC. It was where my experience and skills lay in this context, but having done undercover to the level I did, I have no urge to do it again, except if the project really warranted it for a good cause and it wasn't too long. Since I knew of no projects like that, I thought it was time for change. I had other options becoming available to me that helped me make more meaning of my life.

The meaning making drive within us all could be seen as core to all our social motivations. Being more aware of how we make meaning and what can hinder our meaning making can help us have more authorship of the many pathways we may choose. There isn't one right way to make meaning, but there are many paths that might support our overall wellbeing to a higher level than others (as well as many that don't). Talking and thinking about these can help give us confidence about the path we ultimately take.

CHOOSING OUR OCCUPATIONS

We spend a significant amount of time in our job. It doesn't have to define who we are, but it plays a large part in our wellbeing and satisfaction in life. Choosing a job can be a source of stress, although sometimes we need any job just to make ends meet and the idea of choice is a privileged one. As we strive to find a good level of esteem about who we are and what our skills are, it places a large focus on our occupation. The values of the organisation, the objectives of an organisation and the needs (and personal values) of an individual within the organisation can all be very different things. When they are not well matched, I think this is why our work life can feel disjointed or not fully harmonious. It may be one reason why many of us don't feel an authentic connection between the job we do, what we would like to do and who we feel we are. This is a battle for resilience in our own minds.

At this moment, I felt a disparity between a dominant media culture and how I wanted to be as a person in the world. I was motivated by social good, as were many people I met who were working in the media, but I found it hard to fully square this with an underlying organisational drive and widely held view of some of the public that new programmes, fame/status and high audience figures equated success. I felt the desire to go back to working fundamentally with the principles and values I had when I was working in education, where I felt dominant work cultures fitted more with what I felt was important in life. An opportunity to train as an Educational Psychologist was still open to me and was currently being advertised. I still had the relevant background experience and felt my time in the Army and at the BBC has only enhanced these experiences and developed my views on what it may mean to work towards improving the lives of young people and the systems around them that affect their wellbeing and development. This was another big commitment and challenge as it was a three year training course. I spent some time pondering staying with the BBC or leaving to go back to working in education. I wondered which may provide a better life for me and would enable a future that I wanted. Media work was exciting and varied, but sometimes called for long and unsociable hours. I knew I wasn't driven by reporting on stories and event, but by being involved in them. I wasn't driven by popularising or showcasing a certain type of behaviour, but by attempting to understand it. I knew I didn't want to be caught in the trap of jumping like a puppet into dangerous situations to report what is going on because the organisation I worked for wanted it, but choose in a considered manner which situations I would like to be involved with and if I can make a practical contribution to improving it. I realised I was probably only thinking about staying in TV work because it's 'cool' to have your name on the credits of TV programmes and it can make you feel somehow important when people say 'wow, you were on TV' as if it is some mythical pinnacle of human achievements. I realised that being famous can be a trap whereby you are commodified and have to 'keep up' the elements that make you famous in a stereotypical way for the benefit of making money (often for others) which reduces your freedom and autonomy in many cases. I thought that working in education may often go unrecognised and unrewarded, but ultimately the feeling of knowing you helped (or attempted to help) others improve their lives, even if only in a small way, is ultimately a better reward. Educational Psychology was also my ticket to a more stable occupation in terms of money and working hours, which would tie in more with family life. I thought I may work *with* the media again, but not *for* the media. The mass media is an extremely useful and powerful tool in terms of communication. I thought that although I may never return to this particular lifestyle and occupation, I could potentially work hand in hand with it from a value system and organisational objectives that are primarily focussed on helping others and not on increasing audience figures or profitability. It was time to move on.

Having been so engrained in undercover work at the BBC, not many people believed I was actually going to be an Educational Psychologist. Particularly when leaving Rogue Traders/Watchdog I found approximately 90% of them didn't believe me. This is probably due to the nature of their work. Despite reiterating I was *really* leaving to be an Educational Psychologist, I would still get a nod and a wink as if to say to me 'don't worry, your secrets safe with me'. In my interview to be on the doctorate I got asked a particular question about honesty that I'm sure was testing my real intentions. I couldn't blame people who questioned me about my truthfulness. I realised it's what you do, rather than what you say that allows people to trust you again. I used to deal with sceptical people by pleading my innocence or laughing along to the thought of me being undercover still. On some occasions when I felt it didn't matter what I said, it amused me to act mysterious and let them maintain their doubts. I thought as long as it keeps people working hard and living by the law, what harm does it do if they think I am undercover! People joked about future girlfriends not trusting me and not being able to believe what I say. This didn't turn out to be the case thankfully, but trust has to be earned over time.

I had a BBC leaving dinner with the team that I had become close to during this journey. We had a nice low key dinner at a pub in Notting Hill. The Head of Current Affairs at the time, who was the executive producer, came to show his support. He asked me my reasons for leaving and I told him I was going to become an Educational Psychologist to 'make a difference' and he replied "more than you could with the BBC"? This exchange made me briefly ponder my decision to leave. I never replied as the silence of me thinking was interrupted by others focusing on me wanting to move to be near family and friends in Leeds. The 'making a difference' question is still thought provoking and I feel the media can have a wider, more instant, reach to alter cultures, laws and attitudes in society than working as an Educational Psychologist does. An Educational Psychologist can work in a more targeted and direct way though with children, young people and families without (as many) system restraints and corporate objectives that deflect work from having the most specific impact possible for individuals. In hindsight, I feel I do make more of a 'difference' as an *individual* working as an Educational Psychologist than as an *individual* employed by the BBC due to less hierarchical bureaucracy, increased professional autonomy, training around human development and more targeted organisational objectives on outcomes for improving people's lives. Of course, it does depend on how you define 'making a difference' and it's not simple to do so. Perhaps the question we both should have asked is not if one made more of a difference than the other, but 'how can we make a difference together'?

I see what I tried to do while undercover in the Army as an educational psychologist role, albeit an extreme version. You may ask what an educational psychologist actually does. You would be wise to ask that as it's a bit of a debate within the profession itself. In general, an educational psychologist is concerned with helping children, young people, school staff and families who are experiencing challenges within an educational setting to improve their situation and enhance learning and development. Challenges may relate to social, emotional, or learning needs and be around understanding behaviour. Educational psychologists may work with teachers, parents, young people or a variety of educational and health professionals. Work may involve consultations, observations, assessment of need, implementing a wide range of appropriate interventions, supervision, systems work and training for professionals on a variety of educational and psychological issues. The role isn't straightforward, which is one reason why you have to do a three year training course!

I found it difficult to get back into academia after my time in the Army and the Media. The support of my peers and tutors meant we all pulled each other through the journey of the first year, which is mostly University based. I again went through a period of feeling de-skilled. This was built back up again by the end of the first year.

I see links between investigative journalism and being an educational psychologist. Both are similar to detective work, getting to the bottom of what is really going on despite hearing many different stories and differing views. I see links between Infantry training and being an educational psychologist in terms of developing life skills and a broad education, building groups and dealing with young people with a range of needs. The whole is always greater than the sum of its parts. These three occupational areas are especially powerful when put together. There are examples of them working together. I saw a Panorama programme on February 28th 2011 about retired American soldiers going into teaching. America's

Troops to Teachers programme that helps former soldiers to become teachers has drawn praise for its educational successes. This programme is now in the UK although there hasn't been a high uptake. In February 2011 the government announced a £1.5 million boost to SkillForce, a charity that trains former service personnel to run training programmes in schools, particularly targeting disadvantaged young people.

As people, we can look for links between our values, our skills and our past experiences to support our decision about our current working role. We are much more than our occupational title and if we can find a meaningful way to live our values and use / develop our skills and experiences then we can go some way to shaping how we define our working life and ourselves. This may achieve a balance between enjoying the rest of life and maintaining job responsibilities, while retaining an overall sense of purpose.

FOCUSING ON OUTCOMES

Outcomes have become a main focus in many work areas as well as in education. This can help maintain motivation by being clear about a goal we are working towards and enabling us to think positively and hopefully about the future and how our current actions can affect it. It can co-ordinate people and ideas and bring specificity to what actions people can take to move towards the outcome. This can oppose a focus on some of the 'problems' in discussion that creates low mood and little planning for change. A criticism is that it can narrow our attention away from the process. Being in tune with the present process of our life may be more important than any markers, destination or end point we set for ourselves. An outcome from a situation can be perceived in different ways by different people. It's positive or negative valence can be relative to the individual.

There were several outcomes and changes that I think the whole undercover project contributed to. There were new regulations for the Army and legal implications for specific individuals. There were new ways of doing things and new orders were given. This section looks at some of the outcomes from the project and its effects in court, in the Army and on relations between the BBC and MOD.

Court

In terms of the Corporals who were subject to Military trial, Corporals from R platoon were charged 9 months after the BBC programme. On July 8th 2009, two Army training instructors were found guilty of ill-treating young recruits and fined. Three soldiers told a court martial at Catterick Garrison they were attacked by these Corporals for making mistakes during their training. A military board found both Corporals guilty of three charges of ill-treatment between them after the six-day trial.

They were both cleared of five further counts between them and another corporal and colour sergeant were also cleared of their charges.

One was fined £1,200 after he was convicted of attacking a recruit in a toilet after the young soldier tapped him on the shoulder, mistakenly believing him to be a fellow recruit. The former corporal was also found guilty of kicking another recruit (who has also since left the Army) in the ribs and head for falling behind in a steeplechase exercise.

The other Corporal was fined £600 after he was convicted of pushing the same recruit's head against a door frame.

Assistant Judge Advocate General Paul Camp said he was satisfied the incidents were not "systematic bullying". Sentencing the pair, Judge Camp said they had abused their positions as instructors, who he said are seen as "gods" to young soldiers. The judge described the attack in the toilet on a recruit as "particularly serious" but told the Corporal: "You weren't victimising or bullying the recruits and we regard you as of good character". During the trial, the soldier told the court he had apologised for his error but the Corporal punched and beat "the whole" of his body, saying: "What the f***? Did you just touch me?" The court heard that the Corporal punched the soldier in the chest and arms and bent his finger back, leaving him "in pain". The attack on the other recruit was said not to have caused the soldier any pain or injury.

Addressing the other Corporal, Judge Camp said: "We think you got frustrated. You broke well-known rules and you abused your position as an instructor." He continued: "We want to make it clear that this kind of conduct is not acceptable within the Army and particularly not within a training environment when there is a particularly high duty of care to these young and often vulnerable soldiers". Judge Camp said the Corporal had "difficulty coming to terms with a young man who was not making the maximum of effort". He added that the board did not think the Corporal should undertake a training role until it was satisfied he was not a risk.

In mitigation, barrister David Ward said Army training instructors face “extreme pressure”, knowing the soldiers they train will be going to war. He continued that “Sometimes corporals overstep the mark. It's extremely difficult, but their aim is to make better soldiers who go into the battalion, who have some chance of survival in the plains or the mountains in Afghanistan or Iraq, and some chance of ensuring the survival of those who he works alongside.”

It was a long time before the court case for the K platoon took place. It wasn’t until a year later in September 2009 that I first received a letter to say I may have to stand as a witness in a trial for two of their Corporals. The case was supposed to be held at a Military Court Centre in Catterick in Feb 2010. I was training as an Educational Psychologist at this time, but I did go and meet the BBC team again to check in about this court case. It then got delayed and the charges had not been formally laid out in court by February 2010 and I received another letter saying the court case would be in September 2010, two years after the BBC programme.

In July 2010, I received a short e-mail from the Deputy Court Officer at Catterick Military Court simply saying:

‘Further to my email regarding your attendance at Catterick Court Martial, please note you are no longer required as a prosecution witness and are therefore stood down in its entirety.’

I wondered if that meant it was all over. I wondered if that meant charges had been dropped or they just didn’t want me around for the court cases. The BBC barrister got in touch with the Military Court Service and confirmed that the reason I was no longer required to give evidence was because both Corporals pleaded guilty at the arraignment hearing.

One pleaded guilty to one charge of battery.

The other pleaded guilty to ill-treatment of a soldier and to conduct prejudicial to good order and military discipline.

After over a year and a half of waiting to be called as a witness, I never was. I had mixed feelings about this as I had psyched myself up several times for facing a defence lawyer and seeing the training staff again in person. It was real life and I wanted justice for the young soldiers who had been involved. I also hoped that the hearing was fair on the corporals and that after it was over, everyone could move on with their lives.

There was no BBC response to the convictions and I wasn't asked to do anything else. In the end the court cases passed very quietly. I wondered if this was in most people's interests or if this meant important lessons would be buried. It remains to be seen who was satisfied with what happened and who wasn't.

The Army

I am aware of other changes in the Army since the BBC programme and although I cannot attribute them all to what the Undercover Soldier team did, I believe it was a catalyst for positive change in some cases. See if you make the links (as I do) between the BBC programme and changes in the Army from the following events that are in rough chronological order from 2009 to the present day.

In January 2010, The Daily Mail reported that Sergeants in the Army had been told to adopt a 'touchy-feely' approach. It was reported that the overhaul came after a series of investigations revealed unacceptable levels of bullying in the Armed Forces. Lieutenant Colonel Matt Fensom, said there were 'limitations' to traditional training techniques. He said: "If you are telling soldiers what to do at every stage, a typical command style, what happens when that individual giving the orders isn't there? You can get paralysis. We don't want soldiers to be robots. We need them to think for themselves." Staff Sergeant Paul Campling, 37, from the Royal Tank Regiment added that recruits could still be bawled at if they got an instruction wrong as "There is still a time and a place for a one-way debrief or barked orders but people are happier now because the communication is better."

In April 2011, Ian Drury (who had gone on television to oppose the Undercover Soldier programme) wrote in the Daily Mail of bullying, harassment and racism complaints soaring in the Armed forces. It is debatable if this means incidents have increased or if people now just feel more comfortable to talk about them. There may be many reasons why recruits feel more able to speak out, but I do wonder if the Undercover Soldier programme contributed to this in a culture that discouraged it. In the article it was noted that Dr Susan Atkins, the Service Complaints Commissioner at the time, said the system was 'not working efficiently, effectively or fairly' for personnel. She received 434 complaints from servicemen and women or their families in 2010 (not just related to bullying). This was up from 289 complaints in 2009. Dr Atkins said delays in getting to the bottom of complaints were 'endemic' with 29 unresolved cases dating back to 2005 or earlier. None of the goals she had set for the armed forces were achieved by the end of the year 2013 and her report in 2013 found that of the army's 12% increase in complaints in 2013, only 25% were resolved within the 24-week target and that only 26% of complaints made in 2013 were closed during the year. In 2015, Nicola Williams took over as the service complaints commissioner for the armed forces. The number of bullying complaints specifically was 75, up from 73 in 2012. The total number of service complaints fell by 16%, attributed to the cuts in military personnel numbers. The most recent annual report from the service complaint ombudsman in 2016 suggested 'The number of Service complaints about bullying remained consistent with levels reported in 2015. This was 16% of 890 service complaints (of which 515 were from the Army). It was noted that the Ombudsman believes when read in conjunction with the Armed Forces Continuous Attitudes Survey (AFCAS) from 2016 that this is not a true reflection of the level of bullying, harassment or discrimination in the Armed Forces.'

The Army is also subject to an Ofsted report in a similar manner to schools. In this context Ofsted have a requirement to determine the extent to which progress has been made in addressing issues of care, welfare and support for recruits and trainees during initial training in the Armed Forces. Since the Undercover Soldier project the Army have had Ofsted inspections and reports in 2010, 2013 and 2015. The 2010 report noted that although there had been improvements in some training centres, there had been a decrease in welfare and duty of care provision at a particular training centre - Catterick. This supported evidence the Undercover Solider project had in its prima facie evidence as far back as 2007 and was the teams reasoning for placing me undercover at that particular establishment. In 2010 it rated their overall effectiveness of welfare and duty of care provision for trainees as 'inadequate'. I think the Undercover Soldier programme touched on most of the cited issues and developed a picture from my experiences that was similar to Ofsted's findings in terms of both positives as well as points for improvement. In 2015, the Ofsted report suggested overall effectiveness of welfare and duty of care at Catterick was now 'Good', noting clear improvement since the previous inspections, with some significant changes, including restructuring training programmes and better leadership, welfare staff and management.

Lord Dannatt in February 2011 wanted the Army to give recruits a 'moral education'. Lord Dannatt said that many members of the forces had 'chaotic background' and had not been exposed to traditional values. He said a lack of respect for others could lead to outrages such as the abuse of Iraqi civilians. Lord Dannatt said it was vital that servicemen and women be taught what he called the 'core values' of courage, integrity, respect, loyalty, discipline and selfless commitment. Respect for others, he added, was 'almost the most important' of the values which members of the Armed Forces were taught. He suggested without it, 'that's when you're into bullying or abusing Iraqi citizens'. I agree with moral education being important both in the Army and outside and this links with my previous discussion of values.

In December 2012, a lieutenant Corporal was jailed for four years for trying to kidnap two fellow servicemen while suffering Post Traumatic Stress Disorder. He held one soldier at knife-point at Catterick Garrison, a court martial heard. He then took the man to another soldier's room, where he stubbed a cigarette out on the second man's face. He then fled the camp with one man in the boot of his car after the other managed to jump out and raise the alarm at the guardroom. Our BBC investigation got a back reference in several new reports as it occurred almost exactly four years following the BBC programme release and when five of the Corporals were suspended. These reports also called into question the effects of post-traumatic stress on soldiers and the support and care they receive as well as highlighting the traumatic experience of the recruits in this situation. In the same year the Care Quality Commission found that many doctors and nurses in trauma units for troops do not know how to report suspected abuse cases or how to identify possible victims. The inspections carried out at military bases in the UK and abroad by the Care Quality Commission, at the Ministry of Defence's request - reported that there were no clear guidelines on how to safeguard those vulnerable to bullying. It also found that there was little advice available to soldiers on how to deal with it.

In March 2013, a triple amputee war hero, whose fight to walk again was featured in a BBC documentary ('Wounded') quit the Army after complaining that a senior colleague had bullied him. Paratrooper Corporal Tom Neathway lost both legs and an arm in a booby trap bomb in Afghanistan. In October 2011, Corporal Neathway launched an official complaint that a warrant officer had harassed him over his work. March 2014, saw the Sergeant Major who bullied Corporal Neathway quit his position after an official inquiry found he had singled out Neathway when they worked together at a parachute training school at RAF Brize Norton in 2011.

In March 2014, A Coroner criticised Army chiefs' for their 'unforgivable failings' over the rape case of Corporal Anne-Marie Ellement, who was found hanged in October 2011. The Coroner ruled that bullying, a relationship break-up and work related despair from 'lingering effects' of an alleged rape played a part in the suicide and he called on the MOD to review its care for vulnerable soldiers.

In July 2014, a high court ordered a fresh inquest into the death of Pte Cheryl James at Deepcut barracks in 1995 amid bullying claims. The incidents at Deepcut were a rationale for the Undercover Soldier investigation. In June 2016, a coroner ruled that she died from a self-inflicted shot, 21 years after it happened. This was too late to understand why and for any lessons to have been learned over the past two decades.

Sixteen former army instructors appeared at Bulford Court Martial Centre on September 21 and 22 2017 following a three-year, £1 million military police investigation. The group from the Army Foundation College in Harrogate for 16-17 year old recruits faced a total of 53 charges between them, including ill treatment, actual bodily harm and battery. The alleged abuse included instructors pushing the recruits' heads under water until they choked and forcing animal excrement into their mouths during a training exercise. Some of the instructors are also said to have repeatedly kicked and punched the teenagers, according to legal documents. This has resonance with experiences told to me while undercover almost ten years ago. Six alleged victims were each aged 17 when the abuse was said to have taken place in 2014 during a bayonet fighting scenario in Scotland. All sixteen instructors appeared in court to deny charges. Despite potentially being the Armed Forces' biggest-ever abuse case; it collapsed in court in March 2018 after a judge branded the three-year Royal Military Police (RMP) probe "seriously flawed". The human rights group Liberty said it should be a "wake-up call" for the Ministry of Defence and should force a rethink about the armed forces' system of justice.

It seems there is still something about the culture in Army training, that causes events like these to persist, that is not fully understood. It needs more in depth analysis to increase awareness and more positive outcomes in the future.

BBC and MOD relations

Inevitably the BBC programme has had some effect on relations between the BBC and the MOD. To an extent, both organisations rely on each other to obtain something they both need. The MOD values publicity and public support via mass communication and the BBC values popular subject matter for public consumption.

I wondered how Lord Richard Dannatt really felt about the whole thing beyond his corporate response in the BBC programme. Since the BBC programme, I've seen him compliment the BBC, attack the BBC and use the BBC. He urged the Government to protect the BBC world service in October 2010. He wanted a £272m grant to stay when it was facing cuts from the government because he saw the radio service as a 'relatively cheap' form of communication and beacon of trust for millions around the world including countries where British troops are deployed. He said: 'Expenditure should be protected as fiercely as possible. Both our antagonists and our friends in Afghanistan rely on BBC World Service to find out what is going on. So do our own forces, and millions of other people all over the world.'

He also publicly attacked the BBC in November 2010 accusing them of 'gross insensitivity' for showing a drama depicting bullying among soldiers in Afghanistan. He called 'Accused' (a BBC1 production that centred on attempts to cover up the suicide of a soldier who is bullied and kills himself while serving in Afghanistan) a, 'nasty programme' that should not have been aired when British troops are fighting and dying in Helmand. The BBC received more than 200 complaints about the programme.

In September 2011, almost exactly three years to the day when the Undercover Soldier programme was broadcast, The BBC aired the first episode of 'The Bomb Squad' on BBC One. The Ministry of Defence had allowed the work of specialist bomb disposal teams in Afghanistan to be shown in the documentary. In September 2011, BBC Three broadcast a series called 'Young Soldiers' that was split into four episodes and charted the lives of four new recruits and their families on their journey from day one basic training through to frontline combat in Helmand. The series followed recruits going through training at Catterick and while watching, I recognised many of the locations and training activities. It showed to me that the relationship between the two organisations is still there and there is still an element of trust.

The two organisations also linked up in the documentary series 'Our War' on BBC 3 on the 20th August 2012. The first episode was called 'Into the Hornets' Nest' where 'a daring mission deep into enemy territory is captured on camera by soldiers during Afghanistan's bloodiest summer on record.' I was sat on the sofa at home passively watching the programme that focussed on IED's (improvised explosive device). Suddenly, I heard a familiar voice come through the speaker that resonated in my head and made me sit up straight and look ahead. It was one of the corporals who trained me and was now a sergeant. His face and voice was crystal clear on the TV and he was recalling some of his experiences. Part of me couldn't believe he was on a BBC channel and part of me was intrigued to see him again and hear his stories. Unfortunately, it was a harrowing story and an experience that meant he commanded instant respect for what he had done and gone through. During a firefight in Afghanistan, a comrade was shot in the neck and collapsed into the lap of the sergeant who was filming on a helmet camera. He died of his injuries despite being evacuated to safety. I wondered if the BBC team who had made the new documentary knew that the same soldier had been portrayed a certain way by the BBC before. I wondered if the sergeant had mentioned the Undercover Soldier programme to that BBC film crew and what his feelings were towards the organisation at this point. He had clearly been through a lot since the Undercover Soldier programme and the story presented was moving. It showed the potential reality of a soldier's job and presented the sergeant in a different light - one that was hard to cast a bad shadow on given what he had to do in the line of duty.

In February 2013, the BBC and the Army joined up again through Panorama and had a reporter join allied troops as they prepare to hand over to Afghanistan forces.

It seems the relationship between both organisations is always going to be up and down as they find reasons for conflict and for common ground as their organisational objectives diverge and converge. They are linked in many ways through history and will continue their relationship into the future like brothers growing up together. Hopefully there is a positive outcome for them both.

In supporting our resilience we need a balance of considering possible outcomes in a hopeful manner, while maintaining flexibility in our goals and a focus on the present and the process we are going through. This helps us be motivated by the future, but grounds us in what is happening now and being comfortable with that. John Lennon of the Beatles is quoted as saying:

"Life is what happens to you while you're busy making other plans".

We never know what is around the next corner and this book started off talking about co-incidence. It's good to be prepared, but we can't stick rigidly to one plan. The importance of being mindful in the present is summed up by the Dalai Lama when he was asked what surprised him most about mankind:

"…He is so anxious about the future that he does not enjoy the present; the result being that he does not live in the present or the future; he lives as if he is never going to die, and then he dies having never really lived."

FINAL THOUGHTS

TRAGIC OPTIMISM

Battle can leave us weary, but it can pave the way for new possibilities.

Our battles for resilience as we go through our lives are impacted by many factors at an individual, family, community and global level. In the messy and chaotic state that is our reality, it is impossible to control all these factors to achieve some complete ideal of wellbeing. We will always be at war with ourselves. Some risk and adversity can be positive to help us learn and grow and we can have some choice in how we react to this. We can all strive to develop ourselves and other's wellbeing and the systems that support it as regularly as possible. There are many links that have been made in this book between the BBC, the MOD and me. Many people were connected in some way through the web of making and broadcasting the Undercover Soldier programme. These connections all started because it was an idea whose time had come. An inter-relation of environmental and historical circumstance, co-incidence, individual and organisational cultures and goals at that particular time period meant this project was inevitable.

These chaotic series of interactions also led to the production of this book. I would not have written it if not for all people involved and events that happened before, during and after the actual project. This book, in effect, is authored by every one of those people and it links us all together, as well as you after reading. Some of the people linked in might see what happened as a positive agent for change, some might not.

This story has gone from education, to journalism training, to being undercover in the Army, to being on TV, to working in the Media and back to education again. It has all been underpinned by psychology and an urge to try and understand our brains, our behaviour and our lives. As with most journeys, mine has taken a full circle. Rather than being back exactly where I started, I feel like the experiences have taught me things that I can use positively. Through the ups and downs of the adventure, I feel in a more resilient place to manage the rest of my way through life. I feel I learned many things about myself, culture, business, human relationships and what is important to focus on and strive for in life to feel content on the whole and cope with adversity when it comes along. This is why I always say *"I wouldn't not have done it"*.

Unique stories and circumstances can breed unique opportunities and understanding. Examining the extreme situations we face can often reveal the most about our lives. It took surviving the horror of Nazi holocaust camps for Viktor Frankl[21] to discover the power of hope, optimism and seeking meaning in the face of tragedy. Tragic optimism is the ability to say "YES" to life, despite living and dealing with difficulties, insecurities and threats. It is not unrealistic optimism as a defence mechanism or an artificial over-estimated illusion. It is a way of being that accepts what can't be changed, affirms meaning and value in life, transcends the self, has faith in the future and gives

---

21 Frankl, V. (1985). Man's search for meaning: Revised and updated. New York: Washington Square.

us courage and hope to face adversity[22]. This is something that we can all do in more everyday situations we face. This can help us overcome the battle for resilience.

Three comments through the undercover experience and the aftermath of it have stuck with me:

- **"Everything is finite"**

My current affairs BBC producer strongly urged me to consider that when I had been undercover for months, trying to get filming of bullying and they had no idea when I may get to leave the Army.

- **"After every night time, the sun always rises"**

My Army platoon commander stated that loudly in his battle debrief after our first long and painful combat training session.

- **'One question, at the right time, can lead to positive change'**

My university tutor concluded a key lecture with that during an intense first year on a Doctorate of Applied Educational Psychology.

Following all my experiences, I feel I have an increased understanding for what they were all saying. I choose to believe they have the same underlying important point. I choose to live life appreciating the good moments, being grateful to be alive and optimistic that difficult times will end and can be overcome.

---

22 *Wong, P. T. P. (2007). Viktor Frankl: Prophet of hope for the 21st century. Appears in: A. Batthyany & J. Levinson (Eds.), Anthology of Viktor Frankl's Logotherapy. Phoenix, AZ: Zeig, Tucker & Theisen Inc.*

APPENDICES

STRATEGY FOR DEALING WITH BULLYING IN THE ARMY

If you feel you are being affected by bullying - the following was written as positive steps to take by Bret A.Moore (Clinical Psychologist who served in Iraq), in an article to Army recruits in 2011.

Kevlar for the Mind: Don't tolerate bullies – steps you can take

By Bret A. Moore - Special to Military Times

Being the victim of harassment and bullying is never acceptable. It may seem like your options are limited and that you are helpless to counteract the behaviour, but there are things you can do. It would be disingenuous of me to say that they all work or will work for you. But if you don't try, then you have zero chance of improving your situation.

- Set limits on what you'll tolerate. From time to time, we all have to put up with difficult bosses. Decide when he's crossed the line and take the next step.
- Tell the bully how his or her behaviour is impacting your work. In some cases this is all that's needed. The bully may be embarrassed about making you feel this way or will back off out of fear that you'll be courageous enough to report him.

- Document the behaviour. Write down what you feel is inappropriate. Include detailed descriptions of the behaviour as well as days, times and who was present. This prepares you for the last step.
- Report him to his superiors. In most cases, it doesn't have to come to this. If it does, don't hesitate. I understand that this may be easier said than done. But if you've exhausted all possibilities of handling the bullying yourself, use the military's open-door policy.

THE UNDERCOVER SOLDIER RHYME

This was written by me during my time undercover as a creative outlet to manage and make sense of my thoughts and feelings during this time. I include it here as an example for others to use creative outlets such as rhyme to structure and find meaning in your thoughts and feelings for something important to you.

A year long tale, adventurous steep bids

Full of bangs, plans, silence, violence, soldiers and secrets,

From a job in education to recruit in the infantry,

Metamorphosis, yet somehow, already in me,

Pushing fitness and lessons of extracting information,

Living with an alias, classes of investigation,

They called me David, so who I was would not be known

As I stood before Goliath, clutching a stone,

I could tell nobody the truth, to my safety defend,

The biggest thing I've ever done hidden from family and friends,

I set off to the lion's den, obstacles and pitfalls,

Dreaming on the day that I could tell them all,

Heard that shiver down your spine sound, press up position down,

Stand up, too slow, get your face back on the ground,

Negative reinforcement they called it in the early days

Like lower, raise, lower, raise,

Left right left, marching with blisters for miles,

The long walk, trip and fall or bare it and smile,
Marksmanship principles, I learnt how to aim right,
Shooting targets through my camera or through my rifle sight,
Load a mag, metal click clack, fire, feel the kick back,
Bullet rips the air, shell fell where my feet at,
In a different platoon, I heard of some grave incidents,
So I had to bump into them like it was just co-incidence,
I can't speak during the day so, watch for repetitions
At night, scour camp, eyes flashing for recognition,
I stand at ease there, clutching a camera and a pen,
Alter ego, misdirected, I focus looking at them
And travel in my mind's eye to what they can see
and show them
I'm a solider trying to manifest the 'be the best' slogan,
Gadgets, codes and cameras, thinking spy life is glamorous,
Undercover secrets wild, shooting James Bond style,
But when it's known by you only, life is very lonely,
Mind and heart fractures, creeping thoughts, fearing capture,
It's like a matrix of morals and media, pyrotechnics,
Ethics, calculated steps through geometrics,
Training has to be tough, but they weren't learning enough,
So I was told by recruits, who were having it rough,
They say they couldn't concentrate towered over by the figure,
Sweat dripping off their brow, finger wobbles on the trigger,
From the brain to the arm, energy is eternal,
A fist laid on a recruit, in his memory it burns to,

Some felt hated, reciprocated, recruit bashing,

Undisciplined listening and repeated parrot fashion,

Many played a great role, a few didn't, truly

How can there be duty of care if they don't care about their duty,

Hierarchical, territorial or irrational,

Nature or nurture, local or international,

Never totally protected even with your body armour,

They say what goes around comes around if you believe in karma,

My waking state keeps failing, two jobs in one ride,

Blood shot, heavy, blanking out eyes, adrenaline drive,

Running through the hills, chest howling, heart pounding,

Toll on your soul when you see miles of roads surrounding,

Thunder like tanks rolling, the rain that brings

Grey clouds loom large in the sky like great dark wings,

I'm a rank and a number, forgot my name,

My war face is a mask, over the rough terrain,

In a field far from home barking off testosterone,

Learning animal behaviour while I'm lying in the prone,

Sat under dripping branches, warming hands on a flame,

Weapon cradled on my lap, eating rations, again,

Staring skyward at nothing, wonder what I'm doing here,

Something glistens from my pupil, is it a twinkle or a tear,

As my pulse beat I coped mostly with problems that life lobs

At Christmas hit a wall wishing on going AWOL from both jobs,
Waking up, in the mirror through the sleep in my eye
I saw dad's face staring back at me, emotionless and dry,
Wondering what he would say if he was still here living,
Splash my face, back to reality to the task I was given,
Rifle ranges, running and shooting, marching drill,
Bayonet fighting, screaming kill, kill,
Ironing and cleaning and packing and folding,
Buzzing off attacks at night, no sleep, frozen,
Xbox, headlocks, play pranks and kidding
Food, drinks and posters of scantily clad women,
Through the assault, tiredness, hunger, fighting and noise
It makes you appreciate much more of life's simple joys,
I was a link man in the valley between two of the steepest cliffs,
Felt like a maggot at bottom or an eagle soaring the abyss,
As a recruit I was a crow, as a reporter I was a mole,
Chameleon behaviour when the heat is on the go,
Reflections on a raindrop of a soldier who aims not
To kill, sweeping his sword on the chess board,

People who don't know me, ask me if I changed,
I say no, I've altered slightly but I'll always be the same,
A unique experience I wish I could share with someone else
But how can anyone really understand when I struggle myself,

Thinking back on what I been through, mud on my
black boots,
Ducking down, rolling round ground where these men shoot,
An undercover soldier infiltrated Catterick Garrison,
Seeing the world in ways to which there's no comparison,
For my loved one's who I kept in the dark, please forgive me,
Memories, when I close my eyes, forever in me,
To those who supported me, depths of credit
Appreciate it so much I haven't got the words to say it,
History's employee, chipped in stone on TV,
We number three, the MOD the BBC and me,
Humbly, we all fight for something until life is over,
Even when I'm gone, always an undercover soldier.

If you would like to get in touch with me for any reason following reading this, I can be contacted at:

https://www.facebook.com/BattleForResilience

I will do my best to respond to you when I am able.

www.ingramcontent.com/pod-product-compliance
Ingram Content Group UK Ltd.
Pitfield, Milton Keynes, MK11 3LW, UK
UKHW020224250726
13967UKWH00001B/173